SWEETGRASS MORNINGS

SWEETGRASS MORNINGS

SLIM RANDLES

UNIVERSITY OF NEW MEXICO PRESS

Albuquerque

LIBRARY OF CONGRESS CATALOGING-IN-PUBLICATION DATA

Randles, Slim.
Sweetgrass mornings / by Slim Randles.
    p. cm.
ISBN 978-0-8263-4926-2 (pbk. : alk. paper)
1. West (U.S.)—Literary collections.
I. Title.
PS3568.A537S93 2010
813'.54—dc22
                                        2010015038

For my Catherine

CONTENTS

OVERTURE

───────────────────────────▶

itting here by the fire this night, it seems so long ago
now. I guess that's what happens when you hunt and
fish through dozens of generations of fish and a dozen
or two generations of deer. Only the mountains themselves
don't get older. But look at them, above the fire there in their
black mystery. Maybe they don't get older, but they get a little
friendlier as the years go by. That is because they know us now,
don't they? And we know them. We know the subtle hiding
places of the animals. We know where the secret springs are.
We have walked and run and crawled and sat in these mountains and in hundreds of places like these mountains and now
they are a part of us.

And, what is more important, we are a part of them.

Smelling that smoke drifting up from our fire takes me
back to a late fall day on the very fringes of Seafuse Marsh
in Michigan. I was hunting with my friend George Cornell
on eighty acres of trees and swamp he owns with his brother,
Tom. It was a different hunt for me. Different country: flat,
for one thing, despite all the trees. And different animals.
We were after whitetail deer, which was certainly new to
me, as I'm a child of the West, a man of more open country,

whether in Alaska or California or New Mexico. I had been a hunting guide in both Alaska and New Mexico, and this was new. Each tree was new. The birds were different. Just being here carried with it an exotic theme, and we stood outside George's camp trailer there in the predawn with just a hint of fog rising off the marsh, and George brought out a twisted braid of sweetgrass and without saying anything, lighted the end of it. He blew on it several times to get it smoking, and then, in the tradition of his Ojibway people, he held the braid for me as I fanned the pungency into my face, and my hair, and I pulled the smoke into my chest, into my heart. Then I held it for him as he did the same.

Purity. That's what we sought. We wanted to sink into the magic of the smoke and have it take away all our impurities and our blemishes and the workaday cares of being a writer, in my case, and a college professor in his. We wanted to slip quietly back to a place where our many grandfathers had been, in the foggy woods on a morning like this one, pulling the sweetgrass smoke into our souls and making us hunters again.

Up north in the Athabascan villages of Alaska, the people believe that if you have lived the previous year in a manner that brings you honor, and you therefore merit a moose, you will get a moose. I've always liked that. Earn a game animal by living right and being right with others all through the year.

Well, George and I had done our best through the year, but there were still those little things, the little slips we make, the unkind words we sometimes utter, and the unkind thoughts we sometimes send into the ether. For those, we had the sweetgrass. We have pulled this ancient ritual itself into our very bones and being and hope that will be enough to wash away our impurities so we can have a good hunt.

I've purified my thoughts and hunting abilities now in four states by using sweetgrass in the mornings. I've asked for, and received, its blessings of rich reward on the hunt. Sometimes the reward isn't several hundred pounds of meat, either, but maybe just the sight of the sun greeting the new day through frosty greenish light in the east, or a family of coyotes playing, or being able to say quietly to God thank you for letting that bear pass me by. Maybe it's the singular precious moments of sitting with a rifle or a bow and waiting with that wondrous anticipation, and letting us feel we are home again.

May the sweetgrass of life cleanse you, dear friend, and bring you back to this fire often and with new stories to tell.

—Slim Randles

THE DAY THE
MOUNTAINS
FLIPPED OVER

▶

I met Johnny when he was on the brink of getting old. His face was lined with laugh wrinkles, and his naturally black hair was now shot through with gray. We were guiding hunters together on the northwestern slope of the Alaska Range. It's a strange country, not to be taken lightly . . . a place of extreme distances, extreme weather. A place of large, dangerous animals.

We'd been camped together in this spike camp for more than a month now, and were getting to be pretty good friends. The boss would fly in some hunters, one for Johnny and one for me. We'd help them get their animals and then see them off. Sometimes the next hunters came in on the same plane that took the previous hunters out. Sometimes there was a lag of a few days. During those days Johnny and I would climb to the top of a tundra-covered mountain and glass the immense valley below for game. This was a treat for us, because we had all the fun of looking for moose and bear and sheep, and we knew we didn't have to wear ourselves out trying to get close to them, and we didn't have to further tire ourselves by carrying loads of meat and hides on our backs to the airstrip to be sent back to main camp.

It was during one of these days that we saw the optical illusion, and it affected both of us very strongly. It had snowed recently, making the sky a dull grey mirror and turning all the valley below white. Far off across the lonely reaches of the Kuskokwim River itself lay a low range of hills known to mapmakers as the Pipestone Mountains. These were strange mountains to be found in Alaska, because they were what are called mesas in Arizona and New Mexico. They were flat on top and looked as though they really needed some cactus growing on their sides.

The Pipestone Mountains, though, were a healthy hundred miles or more away from our place on the lookout, and we weren't paying too much attention to them. Some moose that were only three miles away had us focusing on them with the spotting scope. But then Johnny said, "Look at that," and pointed.

The Pipestone Mountains had flipped upside down on top of themselves in our vision. Through some atmospheric magic, these lonely frozen far-off buttes had a mirror image of themselves sitting on top of them, so they stretched their canyons straight into the sky until they blended into the grayish massing of clouds above.

I said to Johnny, "I've never seen anything like that before." He nodded his head. "I've seen some strange things," he told me, "but this one is sure different."

I had a camera with me and took some pictures for the full fifteen minutes this bizarre illusion lasted. The pictures didn't come out.

NIGHT OF
THE COUGAR

The horse was gentle, and so was the pack mule. I knew
their selection had been deliberate. I also knew this
was a test, one of many I would receive in my life,
but a vital test for me, because not every sixteen-year-old high
school kid can be a real eastern High Sierra mule packer, and
I knew it.

At sixteen, having trained for this moment on a number
of pack trips into the backcountry with professionals, I was
now on my own for the first time. How I did in the next two
days, when I returned to the corrals on Sawmill Creek, would
say a lot about whether or not I could be trusted with the welfare of human beings and livestock in a largely vertical and
hazardous country.

Gene Burkhart took a stick, there at the corrals, and drew
in the dust. "Here's Woods Lake. You've been there before. So
you remember right here where that creek comes down off the
pass into the lake? The backpacks are at a camp right where
that creek empties into the lake. You got it?"

"Sure, Gene. I know right where that is."

"You check those shoes often. No barefoot stock, OK? Got
your shoeing kit? OK. Don't turn your stock loose until after

dark. Put hobbles on Brownie . . . and the bell. Turn them loose the other side of the creek. Leona's a good mule. She'll stay with that bell all night. You listen for that bell. You don't hear that bell, you get up and go find your stock. You don't, it's a long walk home."

I stood there, nodding and nodding and wanting to get into that saddle and leave. For Pete's sake, what kind of idiot did he think I was? Hadn't I practiced for this the whole time I'd been there? Hadn't I worked toward this end all summer long? Hadn't I done all the cruddy jobs and milked the goats and picked apricots and fixed fence and learned to shoe and to pack, and fed the stock and stacked hay, and . . . I was about to frustrate myself into a little pool of ruined teen there. Never could stand in one spot too long, anyway.

"I'll be fine, Gene. Honest."

He looked at me. "You got your grain for the animals? You got your hobbles?"

I nodded twice.

"Well, get on your horse and get going. I'll see you tomorrow around three."

At last!

I got on Brownie and picked up Leona's lead rope and rode off away from the corrals into the sagebrush where the Owens Valley meets the vertical massif that is the High Sierra. I looked back and waved once, but Gene wouldn't wave. He didn't do things like that. He just lit another cigarette and looked to see if the horse and mule had their shoes on, as though I hadn't just checked that half an hour earlier.

This was it. I was on a horse, leading a mule. It was only one mule, and it was a dog-gentle mule, but it was a mule with a pack on her back holding my sleeping bag. I was going into the mountains, alone, and was going to spend the night up there with my stock, alone. It was early September, and most of the families had caught their fish and driven back to L.A. to put the kids in school. In a couple of weeks, we'd take some deer hunters up the hill to the meadows where they could try their luck, but right now, we were kinda between customers, or "dudes" as we called them, and could slow down a little. That's why I was allowed to do this trip.

I wasn't the only newcomer to packing at the pack station. There was another kid my age who had been working hard and learning the best he could. He wasn't going to go into the mountains. I knew it. He knew it. Everyone knew it and everyone knew why. He couldn't think well enough to anticipate a problem and head it off. He'd had a few problems handling stock and equipment, problems that were known as jackpots ("He got hisself into a little jackpot up there on the sand hill . . .") and hadn't done well.

For him, there would be chores for the rest of the season, and he probably wouldn't be back next summer. If he did come back, it would be as a chore boy again, and not as a packer.

Thinking reasonably and responsibly wasn't how I really wanted to go through life, either. I yearned for bronc riding, and swashbuckling, and wild horse hunting, and the action all teenage boys look for. You know how it is. I wanted to run wild through the mountains with my nostrils flared out, I wanted to save just one beautiful maiden from the clutches of a biker gang. I wanted to have one of those giant packers from up at Bishop dare to say anything disparaging about the quality of people working for Sequoia-Kings Pack Trains. The minute that happened, I would willingly fling all of my 135 pounds into a vengeful fighting force that maidens would have to make up songs about years later, and I could picture the glory of it . . . telling all those nurses in the emergency room just what a he-man stud-horse wild-ass packer I was.

But that's in an ideal world, of course.

Having to look at a situation and say, silently, okay now, what if I get over this little rise and there's a backpacker and he spooks my stock? What will I do? I'll try to slow down just as I get to that rise so I can see over it before the stock does. That should do the trick.

As I said, I didn't want to do that, but I did want to be a packer. I wanted to be allowed to take a dozen big animals over vertical mountain passes in nasty weather and have Gene and Lona Burkhart back at the pack station know I would get them home all right. I wanted that responsibility and that reputation enough to fight down any impulsive thoughts and start to rationally plan what I would do if something went wrong.

Many years later, I won two mule-packing awards in Albuquerque, New Mexico. Lots of fun, of course. But if you asked any of us who were packing at the state fair, we'd have gladly told you that a timed contest to see who could throw sleeping bags and camp gear on a pack mule and lash it down the fastest is not the test of a champion packer. It's fun, though, and it's fun for the people to watch.

A true champion packer is one who gets his dudes and his stock in and out of the mountains safely, season after season. It's just harder to watch, and to judge. What a good packer does isn't really visible to anyone, including the people traveling through the mountains with him. What a packer does is only visible when he doesn't do the right thing. And being a good packer is just something you know inside.

Was I going to become a good packer? As I rode Brownie away from the remote corrals, and saw Gene drive the stock truck back down toward the highway, I knew I would know by this time the next day. That's why my head was full of celebration and fear at the same time. Could I remember all the things I needed to do? I checked for shoes every hundred yards as we went up the Sawmill sand hill. I checked them that often at first, anyway. Farther up the mountain, I became more sensible and knew checking them two or three times a day was probably good enough. Besides, shoes usually come off incrementally, with a few nails pulling out of the hoof wall first, meaning you have a shoe hanging onto one side, flopping around and banging on rocks for a while before giving up the ghost. But I was so dedicated this day, I was almost wishing one of them would come off, just so I could prove I could put it back on.

As we topped the sand hill, there was a snake in the trail. But then, it seems there is always a snake in the trail, or next to it, right where the trail tops over into Sawmill Canyon. It's a really snaky place. Several years later, one afternoon when I wasn't paying attention, the horse I was riding stepped on a rattler at just that same spot and came close to dumping me on top of the snake. It didn't do the snake any good either.

But I knew about the rattlesnakes of the sand hill, so I stopped Brownie and let him blow some snot at the snake, and in a minute the snake went about his slithering business and we went on up the canyon.

Brownie and Leona and I enjoyed getting into the shade of the pine trees down along the creek, and we all enjoyed a good drink. Then we rode past the ruins of the sawmill and up to Sawmill Meadow, where we stopped for lunch.

Maybe it was because of this trip that Sawmill Pass and Woods Lake became my favorite venues in our section of the High Sierra. Maybe it was because I later packed my dad into Woods Lake and we had some days together and a lot of fun. At any rate, we took our dudes over five outside passes into both Sequoia and Kings Canyon national parks, and Sawmill became my favorite. Years later, as editor of a national magazine, I borrowed a horse and mule from Gene and went up and camped at Sawmill Meadow in the Inyo National Forest during deer season. Took a rifle along. This came after many years of guiding hunters in California and Alaska, but to tell the truth, I didn't care if I killed a deer or not. I was in Sawmill Meadow again, listening to the bell on the horse at night, being alone with my thoughts and my rifle during the day.

But this day was my first day being alone in Sawmill Meadow for the lunch break. I loosened cinches and watered the stock really well, and then checked their shoes again. Right and tight. I had to do this right, you see. It was as if my whole future depended on those two animals having iron on their hooves each day, and not getting saddle sores, and we all stayed healthy and happy and brought back those two backpacks the hikers left in there so they wouldn't have to carry them out. This kind of pack trip is known as a dunnage haul. And, in a very real way, my future did depend on that day and that night and the following day, because if things went wrong, my life would be different. This trail I rode had a fork in it, and checking those shoes was one way of deciding which fork my life would take.

After lunch, we got back on the trail and went up the switchbacks to Sawmill Lake, then climbed above timberline into the scree slopes and bitter winds of the pass itself. Crossing the rocky crest of the Sierra, we were at last able to look down on the large blue gem that was Woods Lake, sitting above 11,000 feet elevation there below us.

Resting the stock in the rare air at the top of any pass is breathtaking and fun, but only for a couple of minutes. After a couple of minutes it becomes cold and miserable, so we rode on down the other side to the lake.

We had the whole place to ourselves. We had seen no one on the Sawmill trail, and when we got to Woods, there was no one there, either. We found the two backpacks all packed up and ready to go at the dudes' campsite, so it would be a fairly simple matter to load them up the next morning. I unsaddled and got a fire going and tied Brownie and Leona to trees and grained them, slipping the makeshift gunnysack *morals* over their heads.

Then I sat on a rock and thought to myself, what should I do now?

The first thought was . . . nothing. I had half my trip completed. I got here with eight horse and mule shoes still hanging tightly to hooves. No saddle sores, happy stock, and everyone having fun.

But then I started my eastern High Sierra packer logical mind going again. When I load those two backpacks on

Leona in the morning for the trip out, will they be balanced? Do they weigh the same? One was for a man, the other for his wife. So I went over and lifted each one, and sure enough, one was at least ten pounds heavier than the other, so I opened them up and took some stuff out of one and put it in the other until I couldn't tell the difference in weight.

Good.

Now I sat down on a rock and looked at the fire, and cooked something to eat and waited for dark.

It took forever.

It wouldn't have been bad if I'd had a fishing rod and could have terrorized the trout a bit, or if there had been dudes there in camp to talk to. Brownie and Leona quickly tired of my stories and dozed off, tied to the trees. No appreciation there.

I hadn't brought a book along to read, which I remedied on future lonely trips. We learn as we go.

But finally off to the west, the sun was sucked down by the unseen San Joaquin Valley and left our little camp in just the comfortable light of the little fire. When it was full dark, I hobbled Brownie and buckled the bell around his neck, and turned the two of them loose to graze. They dingy-dinged off around the lake for maybe fifty yards to some good meadow grass and I settled into my sleeping bag and looked up at an unbelievable sky. I dozed off with the dinging of Brownie's bell telling me each time he grabbed a mouthful of grass.

Then I heard it. It was a screaming. A screaming, a gravelly choking sound, and then a kind of mournful lament combined with a threat. I came flying out of that sleeping bag and pulled my boots on, standing there in my underwear ready to . . . to do what? Okay, my logical eastern High Sierra packer mind told me, you have to think about this. That reasoning official packer thinking was just below the surface. But the immediate thought coursing through my brain was more on the order of WHAT THE HELL WAS THAT?

Mountain lion. Had to be. I'd never heard one before, except in the movies, but that had to be what it was, and I'd heard other packers talk about it. Rocky was talking about it in the bunkhouse one night.

"It sounds like some woman screaming her head off and then getting strangled."

Yeah. That was close enough, Rock. Thanks.

Okay, logical mind. What to do? Well, a cougar's favorite meal of all time? Think, there'll be a quiz at the end . . . horsemeat!

That's right. And what do you have complete charge of out here where there are no adults to help you think? A horse and a mule. And are you going to let that cat eat Brownie and Leona? Hell no!

So I finished dressing by putting on my hat, and turned to go find my stock, but they had beaten me to the punch. Just as I was about to go after them, here they came. I heard this frantic ding-ding-ding as Brownie hopped like a rabbit in those hobbles and he and Leona came into camp and came up to me as I stood there in boots, hat and Fruit of the Looms. They wanted hugs. So I hugged them. I walked over to the fire and they walked with me. I kicked the fire back to life and added some wood so we could see our little world, which extended from that rock pile back there to the tree there against the lake. I walked back to my sleeping bag and they went with me.

I gave up any idea of sleep, got dressed, and pulled on a jacket and heated up some old coffee. If Brownie and Leona had been coffee drinkers, they would've had a cup with me. This was beginning to look like a rather ridiculous scenario.

I tied them to a couple of trees for just a few minutes, because there was something I had to do. I took the flashlight and walked a short way down the lake beach until I found a piece of firewood that was approximately the heft and size of a Louisville Slugger. I took it back to camp. Both animals fussed considerably during the two or three minutes I was gone.

So I got back to camp, sat by the fire, and had my club handy. I took out my sheath knife and laid it next to me. This was a national park, of course, which means no guns, but in those days I didn't own one anyway. But I looked at Brownie and Leona, and they wanted to be with me, instead of twenty feet away. So I got up and untied them. They came and stood on either side of me.

Truth be told, I wanted them next to me, to give me some sense of security, too. I knew they could probably kick the bejesus out of a mountain lion if they had to. I also knew there was zero chance of a lion coming into a camp with a human being and two large animals and a fire going. Cougars seldom get that hungry or stupid. And, since I was sixteen at the time, I hoped that lion wouldn't be foolish enough to come up against this formidable trio. I had my club. I had that sheath knife out and lying right there on the rock next to me. I'd slash that sucker to ribbons before he got my stock!

Something else happened to me that night. Oh, we didn't hear the cougar any more. He'd had his say and had gone looking for deer or a marmot or something. But Brownie and Leona looked at me, and occasionally walked two steps to be next to me and snuffle my shoulder or ear. We became a little middle-of-the-night, middle-of-the-High Sierra family for a few hours, and they made me the daddy. I kinda liked it.

At one point, I was sitting there dozing off to sleep when Leona snuffled my right ear and I set the world's record for the sitting broad jump for packers camped at more than 11,000 feet elevation. I scared myself and both the horse and the mule, and I must have terrified that cat, too, as he stayed away beautifully all night.

But the special thing that happened that longest of black nights at Woods Lake was the realization that Brownie and Leona looked to me for protection. Me. Skinny high school kid. Me. Terrified out of my socks. Me. Must wear corrective lenses. Me. Kid with club and knife. Me . . . packer.

I became a packer right then, I think. The animals knew to come to me. They were counting on my doing what was best for all three of us. They were depending on me to get us all back home again. That's what really happened that night.

After the longest night in the history of civilization, I grained the stock, checked the shoes, saddled them, packed the two backpacks and my largely unused sleeping bag on Leona, and we headed back over the pass. We were at the Sawmill corrals two hours before Gene came to get us.

He looked to see that all the shoes were on, saw the two backpacks hadn't been torn up, and just nodded.

"No trouble?"

"Nope."

"Hungry?"

"Sure."

The hamburger he bought for me that day was eaten by a packer: me.

NIGHT FISHING ON THE STANISLAUS

⟶

There was a time, a lengthy time, a time that seemed to stretch to the breaking point of people, when my wife was hospitalized and I was working full time as a magazine editor and taking care of our two kids, ages three years old and one month old. It wasn't a happy time, there in the little bucolic farming town of Oakdale, California, but it had its bright moments, nevertheless.

On the plus side, I had two of the easiest kids in the world to care for, including our newborn son, who always seemed to be happy, no matter what else was going on. Our daughter was always cheerful and helped with dishes, and each morning took it upon herself to stand on a chair and mix Instant Breakfast for us before the two of them went to day care.

This was a very long time ago, of course, as that little girl, Kyra, is now a grandmother, but sometimes in memory it seems like just last year.

When a family friend offered to come stay with the kids overnight to give me a break, I believe I yelled "Thank you!" as I dashed out the door with my fishing rod and some sandwiches. One must be careful never to give a volunteer time to rethink her offer.

So it's dark, and it's summer in a San Joaquin Valley farming town, and it's hot with that humidity that hangs on you like a blanket, and you don't have to be back until it's time for Instant Breakfast in the morning. It was the wrong time of year to take the hounds out after coons, so the answer was fishing, and the question was where.

Several blocks from our home, the Stanislaus River winds its way through moss-choked boredom on its way to a soft merger with the Pacific Ocean a hundred miles away in the delta. Forty miles upstream, it is a good-sized creek, tumbling over rocks as it cuts its way through the gold rush canyons of antiquity. But just upstream about ten miles is Knight's Ferry, a mini-community centered around a very old and well-photographed covered bridge, built 150 years earlier by Ulysses S. Grant's brothers-in-law, the Dent boys.

And just downstream from the little community, the river runs through rocks and pools and quiet areas, broken only by the occasional dirt roads that leave the pavement and give people access to the slow river for daytime picnics and night-time trysts. I took one of these and ended up along the river, alone, with crickets hailing my visit, and a darkly swirling river to share my thoughts.

This was long before I discovered that there is only fly-fishing and that everything else is just killing fish. These were the days when I had a spinning reel on a short rod, and the hooks in the tackle box could accommodate both worms and salmon eggs. Fishing without thinking. Fishing the way Huck Finn did it.

In a pile of huge rocks directly above the river, I built a small fire and toasted sandwiches as I cast my contribution to trout welfare into the dark waters.

Normally, my energy level wouldn't let me just sit and relax. I have to do something. But that was normally, and these weren't normal times. We both know that going fishing was simply an excuse to be alone in the rocks on a warm summer night and listen to music in my head and not have to think about other things. I made coffee and drank it straight and black, unlike my usual doctoring with sugar and cream. But it tasted special that night, raw and hot, as I contemplated the realities of my life at that time. Drinking it black, I told myself, was a sacrifice I made to flavor and comfort, as though that would help my very selfish prayers be heard more easily. See the man deliberately making life hard on himself by drinking coffee straight. Please pay close attention to his plight.

But the plight had to take a backseat to just being there. Just being next to a fire, as I fed sticks into it, keeping it hat-sized through the night. It threw just enough warm light on the rocks at my back to keep me warm in a cocoon of light and natural love. I looked down occasionally the ten vertical feet to see if that bobber was jerking around with a suicidal trout attached to my hook. But as the night went along, I looked down less and less.

I recall making it a matter of honor not to look at my watch. Why should I? Does it matter what time it is? No. I'm here on a rock above the Stanislaus River on a warm summer night, being serenaded by nearly every cricket God ever made, and the occasional owl. I really tried to concentrate on the night and the fire and the fishing and the coffee and the sandwich. With everything I had, I wanted not to think about the illness my wife was going through, not to wonder when, if ever, she would be with us again. I tried not to think about those little kids at home, or to speculate whether I would be father enough to take care of them and raise them alone if those were the cards life dealt us.

But there are only so many times you can look down at the bobber or check the fire. And when I looked up at the stars through the heat haze of a valley summer's night, those other things came back to haunt me.

So the night went along, with the trouble ghosts hanging on my shoulders. The questions asked by the owls went unanswered because I didn't know the answers. We never do. All we can do is our best with the cards we're dealt.

When there started to be definition to the trees around me in the pre-dawn morning, I sat there, wide awake, without any of the fatigue one might've thought would be party to an all-nighter on the river. The trees became more and more visible and the fire died down and I let it. I brought some water up from the river and poured it on the fire and just sat there another minute before calling it a night.

Then the bobber bobbed and I reeled in a six-inch trout.

I let him go and drove home.

Thirty Feet
from Death

Y ou were asking me about close calls. Most any guide
has had a few, if he's spent any time at all in the bush,
and I guess I'm not an exception. I had one black bear
die just eight feet from my boots, which was probably the closest I ever came to being killed by a bear.

But if you're interested in strange stories, and if you have a
few minutes, I have one that is strange, very strange. And it's
true, too.

It was many years ago now, of course. It had been a good
fall, with lots of moose and sheep for our hunters. I was guiding
for Clark Engle, who was a wonderful guide and a real character as well. We all enjoyed Clark's penchant for practical
jokes, and he was a fine teacher of hunting to a young guide.

And, oh, was I ever a young guide in those days. I had
experience, and I was a long way from being a novice, but
there are always things to learn in close company with dangerous animals, and we tended to keep our ears open and learn
from the older guides as much as we can.

Still, though, young guides make mistakes. Some of them
only make one mistake and it costs them their lives. I was

lucky. I survived my biggest mistake that fall and I can be here now to pass advice along. But I wouldn't have survived at all if that moose hadn't saved my life.

In those days I was out at Clark's camp on what he called Moose Lake. The lake doesn't have an official name, but it's on the western slope of the Alaska Range between the Swift Fork and the South Fork of the Kuskokwim River. Just a tent there, but it was a nice 12-by-14-foot wall tent, rigged up to be warm in even the coldest weather . . . as long as the fire in the stove didn't go out. It was just the right size for a guide and a hunter, and I stayed there more than forty days that year, with Clark bringing in one hunter and taking out the previous one, along with the meat and trophies.

It was getting late in the season. The first snows had fallen and melted. The moose were quieting down out of their rutting season now. The little weasel that came in the tent each morning for his piece of bacon was turning white and becoming an ermine. The weariness was upon me, too—that weariness that comes after long weeks with everything a man needs except enough sleep. The weariness makes you smile philosophically sometimes at the racket of the red squirrels, and can even make you hear the music of the mountains swelling up from the tundra through your boots and making the lightly yellowed glow of a late fall day sparkle with magic and mystery.

Clark had brought Jim in to me because he had looked for a grizzly in another camp for several days without success. Moose Lake was primarily known as a moose hunting paradise, and Jim had already taken a huge bull in another camp, but I had a grizzly and that's why Clark flew him into my camp.

I had seen this bear almost every day for several weeks. He was a beauty, a chocolate brown grizzly rolling in fat. He'd weigh 750 pounds easily, and was fast. I saw him running along a tundra ridge one morning, not chasing anything, not running from anything, totally unaware of my presence despite my being the only person in that part of the mountain range. I think he was running just because it was fun to run. I've felt like that a few times myself.

Well, I kept seeing him, and I knew he was visiting some of the gut piles where my hunters had killed moose earlier. Those old grizzly bears love gut piles. They don't really like them until they are pretty . . . well, I guess *ripe* is the word. So to keep other animals off their food until it's just right, they'll tear down small trees and root up brush and drag it over the kill, or in this case, the gut pile, to at least protect it from the birds. Wolves and black bears are usually intelligent enough to leave a grizzly's kill alone and go find their own.

So Clark flew Jim into my camp, and we spent the evening getting acquainted. Nice fella, he was. The next morning we set out to check a few of those old moose gut piles to see if we could find that beautiful chocolate bear. We sure were successful, too, and it still makes my heart jump and start pounding on my collarbone just thinking about it.

We checked one pile not far from camp and saw that the bear had come, had dined, and had gone. What scraps were left had been cleaned up by the furred and feathered members of the Rural Alaska Sanitation Department. They do a very thorough job of it, too. Just as we were leaving the kill site, we heard an old bull moose grunting and heading our way. Jim didn't need a moose, but he did have a camera, so I told him to get it out and get it ready and I'd see if I couldn't grunt this bull in close.

Jim got ready and I heard that old bull grunting even closer, maybe fifty yards away in some alder thickets, so I held my finger to my lips to keep Jim quiet, and I grunted that old bull.

What's that like? Well, as animal calls go, it's about the easiest to imitate and you don't need some artificial shiny wooden call that costs too much at Kmart, either. You just grunt really deep in your chest.

Now these bulls walk around a great big area, grunting like that, to attract girlfriends. The cows walk around when they're in estrus, listening to the bulls do their lonely little grunting walk, and pick out the best grunter to be the daddy of their next calf.

You'd think if you were grunting in another bull's bailiwick that it'd make him angry and bring him in ready to fight. It doesn't, though, because moose are only slightly smarter than a pet rock, for one thing, and for another, they are so nearsighted they couldn't catch a train. When you grunt one in, if you stand still, he thinks you're just a tree wearing a red hat.

So we had a little fun calling the moose in for pictures. I grunted, and then he grunted. I waited a friendly amount of time and grunted again, and he walked up to the clearing where we were. He looked at us and grunted again, and I heard Jim's shutter clicking. Then the bull lost interest and wandered on about his business, trying to find his life's love out in the middle of Alaska. Jim and I laughed at the silliness of the bull, to be fooled so easily by my grunting, and Jim said he was pretty sure he got some good photographs of the old boy, and then we continued on our check of the gut piles.

One by one we checked the gut piles. I think there were six or seven of them to check, after several months of very successful moose hunting. That particular area is just packed with moose. On the third gut pile, we heard that old bull coming again. He had made a big semicircle, you see, where we had cut straight across. Jim said he wanted to see if he could get some more pictures of him, so I told him to give it a try this time. He grunted, and it wasn't too bad a grunt for a first timer. That old bull heard it and grunted back politely and came toward us to say hello.

A couple more grunts and here came Old Paddlehead into our clearing. He was a huge old bull, a trophy in anyone's book. His antlers were at least sixty-five inches across, maybe as much as sixty-seven inches. The bases of those antlers were the size of truck axles, and this bull had to weigh 2,000 pounds.

If you saddled him up like a horse, that saddle horn would be seven feet off the ground. So Jim got some more pictures, and the bull wandered off on his quest.

That gut pile had also been cleaned up thoroughly, so I decided we'd better walk a ways and check out the freshest gut pile, where one of my hunters had taken a bull just a week earlier. If that pile was gone, I thought, the bear probably was, too.

Now this gut pile was in the middle of a stand of alders and spruce up the creek quite a ways. You wouldn't be able to tell if it had been worked until you were right on it. Did this bother me? Of course not. Hey, it was a good morning. Wasn't too cold, we'd gotten some good pictures of Old Hatrack there, and we were having fun.

We were walking across some blueberry flats, fairly open country where the bushes are only knee-high, and heading for the trees where this gut pile was. I looked ahead to that part of the stand of trees where I knew the kill to be, and noticed some ravens and magpies sitting in the tops of the trees above the kill.

Did this bother me? No. Why not? Because I was a young guide and wasn't thinking. If I had been an older guide, like older by one day, I would have noticed those birds and asked myself why they were in the trees when there was a feast waiting for them just below. But I didn't. And then we both started laughing, because just as we were about to enter the trees, we heard that same old bull, grunting and heading our direction through that very same stand of trees. We just stopped about ten feet inside the trees and were going to wait quietly for our friend the moose to go on by before going in to check the kill. The kill, I knew, was about thirty feet ahead of us.

We stood there smiling as we heard the moose grunt along into the area of the gut pile, and then it happened. There was a tremendous roaring and thrashing and we heard the bear blow the air out of his lungs in that unforgettable sound that means combat. Jim and I worked the bolts on our rifles automatically, throwing rounds into the chambers, and backed out of those trees so fast I don't think we touched the ground. With our hearts pounding, we stopped about a hundred yards away and waited. But by that time it was all over.

In about 30 seconds, that chocolate grizzly had killed a bull moose who was stupid enough to bother his gut pile. And I knew our grizzly hunt was over, too, at least for that grizzly. Because now he had two kills to guard, and he would camp within a short dash of that dead bull until it became ripe enough to be interesting to him.

The big winners that day were Jim and me. We both lived to hunt again, and we both took with us the memory of one of the closest calls either of us would ever have. If that bull hadn't arrived first, we'd both be dead. And we knew it.

You can see my hands shaking, can't you? Isn't that strange? After all this time, that still gets me going. A grizzly is a terribly efficient killing machine. When you meet him, it had better be on your terms and not his.

The one big regret I have is that I wasn't able to get that bull moose's antlers. I had to leave that camp before the sanitation squad cleaned up that bull. But I wanted to take those antlers home and hang them up to honor him and to remind me that sometimes Mother Nature gives us a pass and lets us learn by our mistakes.

And this is one guide who always, always, checks the tops of trees to see if the birds are there instead of being on the ground where the food is.

IN THE COLD
ALASKA RAIN

▸

It was one of those freezing cold days in late summer and I wasn't happy about walking out through the tall wet grass to catch the train. Alaska has the coldest rain in the world. The rain in Alaska defies every scientific morsel of knowledge or manmade rule. I've seen it snow at 50 degrees and rain at 25. It's as though everything but the dollar bill and the American flag change when you come to Alaska. And this afternoon was one of those.

I was going to Talkeetna on the train from the cabin, and going alone for some reason. Pam and Mandy were staying home where it was warm and dry. It wasn't that different from many other times I'd flagged down the Alaska Railroad where our trail meets the tracks and the Susitna River.

Well, not at first, anyway.

When I reached the tracks and stood between the rails and waited to see that big headlight come around the curve of the mountain, I just stood there, miserably huddled against this rain that penetrated any weak spot in clothing, that saturated any clothing that wasn't waterproof, that stung with cold any exposed skin.

Between where I stood on the tracks and the banks of the Susitna River was maybe twenty yards of cottonwoods and willows. In the early and hot parts of summer, we used to walk out there and sit quietly and watch Vickie's pups play near their den. Vickie (short for Vixen, of course) was a red fox who came to the banks of the river every summer to raise her family. Where she went in winter, we never knew, but every summer it was fun to watch her pups play and grow and become foxes.

Her babies were getting pretty big by this time, and would be on their own soon. There was no sign of them near the den mouth, so I imagined they were all inside keeping dry.

Not all of them, however, and that's what made this particular afternoon special. As I stood looking north up the tracks for the train, I noticed movement between the rails headed my way. Through the pouring, freezing, saturating rain came one of Vickie's fairly grown pups, heading home. This poor devil had his head hanging down, and his usually pretty red fur was now a wet brown blanket, hanging and dripping on him as he trotted quietly straight at me. His eyes were drooping and he obviously didn't see me.

As I watched him come, I thought of how we both shared this misery out here in the middle of a wet and nasty Alaska afternoon, and I thought I'd just stand there, in the center of the tracks, and see how long it would take him to see me.

He just kept coming.

When he was maybe ten feet in front of me, he raised his head and looked at me, and then hopped over one rail and walked past me a few feet, looking up at me the whole time, then hopped back between the rails and headed home.

I don't suppose this is anything much to anyone else, but it was an interesting moment in the lives of a man and a fox. For that little period of time, we were just two guys—two wet, cold, miserable guys—having to live in the cold Alaska rain.

ON BEAVER
POND . . .

⟶

It's a summer evening in Alaska's bush, and the bugs are bugging around and the birds are flit-doodling, and there's that lazy, languid feel in the rank green jungle where we live.

Grown-ups can enjoy the evening by visiting or listening to the battery-operated radio or just reading and doing a bunch of nothing while waiting for it to get dark after our bedtimes. But for a two year old, there just has to be more to life than this. There's no television, of course, and in our particular case, there were no other kids for our daughter, Mandy, to play with. We'd read to her, naturally, but she now had every book in the cabin memorized. She was too little to take fishing, really, so what do you do to entertain a two year old?

Tease a beaver.

Yea, verily, summer evenings were meant to be spent in a laughing torment of the animal with the smallest sense of humor in the bush. Beavers look at the world very seriously. If they have any fun at all during their lifetimes, they're awfully good at keeping it to themselves. They live to work. They work in the winter, they work in the summer. They are like the U.S. Army Corps of Engineers in that they hate to see water move.

If water moves, stop it. That's all. Plug it up. Then eat some bark. Then look around to see if any water dared to move while you were eating that bark. Then plug it up.

If the clowns of this world do bad things while they're here, it would be difficult to find a more appropriate punishment than sending them back to earth as Alaska's beavers.

So off we'd go in the evenings, occasionally, down to the neighborhood beaver pond just as the long twilight is twilighting, and we'd sit quietly by the beaver pond and wait.

Beavers are largely nocturnal. You just don't see them out much during the day. But in summer they have a problem, because there just isn't enough darkness for them to get all their work done. You can't expect a beaver to sit around the old lodge watching television when there might be some water outside that could suddenly *go somewhere*. So beavers will begin emerging from the lodge at twilight, to get a jump on the work to be done.

It's usually Papa Beaver who comes out first. Papa Beaver is hereafter to be known as the teasee.

So we sit quietly, not moving, not even whispering, and we suddenly notice that big V in the unbroken surface glazing of the pond. We look at each other and giggle silently, because this is where it's really going to get *good*, you know?

Before Papa Beaver can give the all-clear for the rest of the family to come out and start working, it is his job to be sure there aren't any predators or other haunts and boogers out there in the pond first. It wouldn't do to have the kids come out and get lunched by a bear.

So here he comes, good ol' Papa Beaver. He swims slowly and silently back and forth, checking each willow clump, each little nuance of Beaverdom as he swims. He watches with his tiny little nearsighted eyes, and he listens with his tiny ears and he swims. And the closer he gets, the more excited we become. But we know from experience that the time has to be exactly right before we can act, so we stifle our natural urges to giggle and laugh and jump up and down, and we wait some more.

Oh man, here he comes! He's only about ten feet away now, but he has to swim across to the other side first, and then come back to us. We know, if we've figured this just right, that Papa Beaver should come within three feet of us if we don't blow it first.

There! He's over at the other side of the pond, and he's turned and is heading back. We grin at each other, and we can feel our skin twitching with anticipation, but we sit still and wait.

Here he comes, slowly, slowly. We hold our breath until we look and can see every hair on his head, every nuance of both his eyeballs. He's going to be close enough we can almost reach out and touch him. The tension is about to do us in.

Then the adults give Mandy the nod, and she leaps to her feet, throws both arms out wide . . .

"Boo!"

Ol' Papa Beaver comes straight out of the water, does a half-gainer with a Sukuhara twist and whams his big flat tail on the surface as a warning to beavers all over the world, and disappears under water. While he does a hurried frog-man swim back to the underwater entrance to his lodge, we laugh and shout and do a post-mortem on the booing and the splashing and we practice making our faces look as surprised as his was when the boo struck home.

For about ten minutes, we are free to rehash the boo and the splash and do the instant replays and the post-boo inter-views. But when it gets close to about fifteen minutes after the first boo, we have to settle down and take our seats again, as the curtain is about to go up on Act Two.

Sure enough. Papa Beaver's little brain has now forgot-ten the scare, and his innate need to stop water has overcome any sense he might have possessed. Here he comes again. And for long, silent moments we do our laughing silently and grinningly in anticipation of the next boo. Back and forth across the pond he goes until he once again is nearly in our laps.

"BOO!"

Oh man . . . I think that one was even better than the first one. Did you see how he arched his back this time?

GOING TO THE
HIGH COUNTRY

————————————————————▶

When the first wisps of cool brush my home in early morning, let me go to the high country. As the valley bakes to a bronze finish in the late summer sun, let me walk where eagles fly on silent deadly searches. Take me up to the cool shade of the evergreens, let me hear the bugling of the elk, the hunting cry of the coyote. Let me cry a little hunter's cry, too. For it is the time of polishing, of refining, of brushing to a slick gloss all the traits that make us the most complicated of animals. It is the mating time, the hunting time. It is the time of golden leaves and soft ground that sinks softly as we step upon it. It is the time of being alert and looking around us and trying the ages-old instinct once again.

It is the time of perfection, that time when the antlers are sharpest, coats are shiniest, teeth are whitest, and eyes see things that may or may not be there.

Let me go to the high country, greet the timberline, slip in and out of the trees, walk the open spaces high above the Dutch oven valleys below. Let me try once more to be the best I can be, to savor life, to sip once again that coffee from the fire, straight as life itself. And though there's no sugar or cream, we know it's the best we'll ever have.

Tell me stories, there by the fire, as we keep our traditions alive with color and beauty and the breathless parts of terror. Let me remember your face as it looks in firelight, and please remember me that way. Let the stories come, polished or plain, true or should-be true. This is our way to be human, to keep going, to let young people know this is how we are and who we are. Because we know, at life's slowing, that the most important thing we did was to make memories with others.

When we walk the high country, the tall high-ups where no motors go, we drink in the quiet like soft wine on a fancy picnic. For a while, a golden special while, we are above everything but life itself. The world may not be ours, but for a while, we are not the world's either. Down in the noise people worry and take pills and look at their watches. For a while, though, we look up only to see clouds and answers.

The world may not be mine, but I am not the world's either, for this moment in time, and that time will stay with me through the cold months of winter, the winds of spring, and next summer's frantic heat. This time of beauty and peace and prayer is my time, and your time, and the high country is home. It is our old home. The old home place we remember only when we are alone and quiet and in that magic time between sleep and morning. In our old home, each canyon is a room, each tree an umbrella, each animal a kindred spirit. And while there, we hear the music of the mountains and the mind. We see the laughing faces of those who are now in far distant camps and will never be in this camp again. We see things and hear things we don't mention to others because to do so would profane the perfection of memory. And when we're there, we'll immerse ourselves in the cleansing bath of air that smells of the perfume of life itself, and be thankful.

Too soon our rooms will be smaller and less beautiful. Too quickly our minds will work on small problems again. But this is our moment, high up here where no one goes except those who would be our brothers and sisters. This is our time. Our moment. We, too, become perfect, even if just for an instant. But that is enough. We know, through the cold and clutter of winter, that we had our perfect moment and we will keep that inside, like a shiny rock in a special pocket. And we'll know. And if we sing a heart song as we look across the mountains, let us be forgiven if it isn't perfect yet. Because inside we know it's meant to be perfect, and the mountains are kind enough not to tell.

Then, when the heart is full, we can go back down the mountain as new souls, full of kindness, and we can each work to find a mate and a place out of the cold to come.

I NEED COFFEE!

→

As a recycled cowboy, it gripes me to realize that for much of my happiness I am indebted to hyperactive sheep.

According to legend, in about AD 1000, sheep grazing in what is now Ethiopia after munching some red berries started frisking about and having fun. The shepherd, named Kaldi, chewed some of these berries, grinned, and said, "Man, I just can't live without my coffee."

Which just goes to show that some things never change.

Coffee, of course, is one of the world's three basic food groups, the other two being barbecue potato chips and corn dogs. Coffee has become so important in our daily lives that the entire Pacific Northwest has come down with a gang addiction. On a recent trip to Oregon, I noticed that every two blocks in all the bigger towns there were drive-up coffee kiosks where you pay four dollars for a cup of coffee that tastes like it was filtered through shredded tires and whose name is unpronounceable. And about the time the breakfast coffee rush wore down (shortly after 2 p.m.) a distinctly Pacific Northwest ritual began known as the p.m. perk. Here came the long lines of cars again, with hands grasping five-dollar bills reaching out the car windows and shaking with the early stages of withdrawal.

Ahh, the bean, the blessed bean. Oh bean, thou art craved in the deepest fibers of our being, thou infiltratest our cellular essence with the sunshine of morning and brusheth away the cobwebs of gloom.

Back when I was guiding hunters in Alaska, I had one German industrialist who couldn't stand the way we made coffee. One morning in the tent, ol' Wilhelm said "You Americans know nothing about coffee . . . out of my vay!"

Wilhelm then filled a pot with water, threw in what appeared to be an equal amount of coffee and fended me off with a three-tined fork until this mess had boiled for about ten minutes. I watched carefully, and my notes tell me that German coffee is done when the white speckles melt off the enamelware pot.

"Dis," pronounced Wilhelm, waving his arms as his eyes flew open, "is COFFEE! Vun cup, you are good for a veek!"

It was strong, all right. We hunted seventy hours straight and had a foot race back to the coffee pot when we finished.

On our ranches we have many different rules. Some ranches don't allow photography, some welcome fishermen, some shun outsiders who want to hunt. But all of them have one inviolate rule: the coffee must go on. There is somewhere a pot of coffee in the house, and if it is empty, it is filled again immediately whether there is anyone to drink it or not. Friend or foe, process server or godfather, Scylla or Charybdis, it matters not.

All are welcome at the caffeinated fount of Western hospitality. You wouldn't even shoot a guy for dumping your daughter without giving him a cup of coffee first.

Coffee was even given a papal blessing back in 1600. There were a bunch of Christians (obviously on decaf) who were petitioning Pope Clement VIII to ban coffee for being the devil's drink. He didn't want to do that without trying it first, being a fair-minded guy, so he had some cardinal whip up a batch and he sucked it down. He gave the drink his blessing, said it was an official Christian beverage, had a mug made with "Clem" on it, and hung it over the sink.

There is nothing on earth like coffee. It gets into the very marrow of our bones and makes us live long and happy and energetic lives.

Decaf, you say? (Decaf should be made legal grounds for divorce.)

Tea? (Point to the globe and show me what's left of the British Empire. 'Nuf said.)

Of course, you can take coffee ingestion to a ridiculous degree. Does the term *blitzkrieg* paint a picture? But for most of us, we take it black, we take it with cream and sugar, we take it any way we can get it, but we take it. It's kept some people moving and writing columns years after they were declared literarily brain dead.

Long live nervous Ethiopian sheep. Please pass the sugar.

SNAKIN' IN
SOME WOOD

⟶

I t wasn't my fault. She was a vision of loveliness in jeans and a western shirt. There's only so much you can expect from a seventeen-year-old packer. Make that a seventeen-year-old official eastern High Sierra packer, which is the pinnacle of packing prowess, after all.

Of course, she brought along her family on this pack trip, which I guess must be expected of most sixteen-year-old visions of loveliness. Daddy was some kind of Los Angeles executive, and he was a nice guy. Her mother was a forty-year-old vision of loveliness herself.

Then there was a bratty ten-year-old kid brother, but we'll skip over him as he really doesn't figure in this most embarrassing mule-packing mayhem.

But the start of the day wasn't mayhemic. She seemed like a nice girl, down there at the corrals at the base of the Sierra. She was pleasant and polite, although not extremely impressed by the fact that I was an actual eastern High Sierra mule packer, pinnacle of . . . well, you know the rest.

She smiled, and my knees buckled. She said good morning, and my heart stopped. She introduced me to her father, and my heart started again and I got down to business.

I tried not to let her know how thrilled I was at being allowed to adjust her stirrups. I actually touched her boots as I slid her feet into the now-perfect-length stirrups. For those who might not be aware, the perfect stirrup length for a long ride in the mountains is enough stirrups to let you stand in the stirrups and have your butt clear the saddle seat by about an inch. Any shorter than that and you'll pay for it later in knees that feel as though Argentina just fell on them.

Now the way things happen when you start out from the corrals at the base of the mountain is that the packer takes his mules and starts up the trail first, followed by the party (known as the "dudes") in no particular order. Now the way things worked, she—make that SHE—got her horse in right behind my caboose mule and let the rest of her family string out behind her.

This may not seem important, and it probably wasn't, but that's not taking into account the internal thinking of a seventeen-year-old eastern High Sierra packer. Oh no. What is going on in his mind are variations on a theme: "Did she get behind my mules just so she could be closer to me?" "Is she attracted to me in some way?" "Is it the fact I changed my shirt this morning?" "Does she want to be closest to me in the family so she can hear whatever pearls of official eastern High Sierra packer wisdom I can pass along?"

Naturally, I voted for all of the above and set sail for the crest of the Sierra Nevada with a heart as light as butterfly hemorrhoids. At this moment, my thought processes were running along the lines of "I'd just like to take a little nip on the left side there, and then get lockjaw and let her drag me to death."

Of course, I didn't get to say anything to her, really, until after lunch at about 9,000 feet elevation when we hit the "steps" or the tight switchbacks. On this part of the trail, the country gets so steep it'll cause a mountain goat to wet himself, but it did something else, too.

It gave me the opportunity on the switchbacks of looking down at her and saying something to her. This was a challenge, because in the steps you hit a switchback about every two minutes. This means I not only had to think of something to say, but it had to be good. You know.

I wanted her to ponder my pearls of packer wisdom for the entire two minutes it took her to reach the next switchback, when again I'd be within talking range.

At this point, it's only fair to point out that I've never really been the strong, silent type. I've always been more the weak, noisy type.

Years later, one of my clients in the High Sierra wrote this poem about me: (revealed reluctantly here for the first time in print in the interest of truth and the American Way)

> Slim talked and talked to the silent sphinx
> Who answered him not,
> Said Slim "He stinks!"
> Slim rode for an hour in Echo Canyon
> Singin' and talking;
> Talkin' and yellin'
> An answer came back from every beller,
> Said Slim, "Damned agreeable feller."

Unfortunately, that poem is more accurate than I usually care to admit. So I thought I should have some kernel of magnificence to pitch at her on every switchback.

I wasn't enough like John Wayne to just squint my eyes and smile at her and expect her to melt into daydreams of having my children. Oh no. I was a skinny cowboy wearing glasses and growing a scraggly beard that failed miserably in its attempt to make me look twenty-five.

So I had to say something to her on each switchback that I hoped would make her get to camp and say, "Darling, let's me and you ditch Dad and go behind a rock somewhere and play slap and tickle."

So I tried to think of impressive things to say to her. These were one-liners, of course, out of necessity. You just aren't in conversation range for that long, you see.

So my little gems of high country seduction included these:

"These ol' mountains sure get steep, don't they?"

"Your stirrups comfortable?"

"You like school?"

"You like ol' Tiny Man there?" (Tiny Man was her horse.)

"Be at the lake before too long."

"Getting hungry?"

"Me too."

On each of these, about all she did was smile and nod.

If I thought she'd keep up that smiling and nodding, I might have asked her more intriguing questions. Questions like "Do you find packers attractive?" "Would you like to bear my children?" Stuff like that.

Looking back on it now, I'm certain she actually had a voice, but I didn't really give her time to use it. I was determined to make her weak in the knees with my pack-station palaver so she would dream of being held in my skinny arms and worshipped as was her due.

Before I ran out of things to say on the switchbacks (just before) we reached the high country lake that was our goal, and I unpacked while the family set up camp. I unsaddled everybody and tied the stock to trees to wait for dark. At dark I'd hobble the bell mare and turn everyone loose on grass, but for now I didn't have much to do except give everyone grain and check for any loose or missing shoes. Everyone was fine.

Her daddy had a fire going and coffee on and I went into camp and grabbed a cup of it and squatted near the fire as the sun headed west for Fresno.

It was unearthly quiet. In later years, it occurred to me that this was actually what this family was looking forward to, but at that time, I was the unassailable force sent to shore up any discomforting spells of silence. I was really good at it, too.

I looked at her. "You know," I said, "I think I'll just snake in a little firewood for you folks."

She smiled and nodded. She did that a lot.

"Yes," I said, remembering what Will James wrote about, "that's what those old-time cowboys did, you know. Snaked in firewood. I mean, you could always go out there and carry it in on foot, but that's the hard way. Snakin' it in. That's how they did it in the old days."

Her daddy was giving me a weird look, but I wouldn't be stanched by such as that.

"Think I'll take ol' Tiny there, your horse. He'll be good for snakin' in wood."

So I threw a saddle on Tiny Man, a fourteen-hand (that's pretty short) mustang who started his career as a wild horse in the Coso Mountains. He was about the gentlest thing on four legs in the Sierra.

I built a loop in my rope and rode ol' Tiny up the hill from camp about fifty yards where I found a big ol' snaggy piece of firewood, with sticky-outy arms protruding from it. It looked likely, so I dabbed a loop on it and turned ol' Tiny towards camp.

Well, Tiny Man may have been the gentlest kid's horse in the mountains, but he never was a roping horse. Swinging the loop made him a bit nervous, but he was a good guy and took that in stride. When I turned him towards camp, and that nylon rope came tight between the saddle horn and the firewood, he got a bit more nervous. He danced a bit and snorted as the snag started down the hill behind him, but ol' Tiny was a pardner of mine and I knew he'd be all right.

That vision of loveliness was sitting down at the fire, smiling and watching me, probably already planning how to announce our engagement.

So Tiny snorted and danced and stepped sideways, but he kept going downhill. Until we hit that rock.

Well, we didn't hit the rock, but that snaggy piece of firewood did. It caught behind that rock and just hung there. I goosed Tiny Man with the spurs and he leaned into it, trying to pop that snag loose. That nylon rope stretched just like a big ol' rubber band. I smiled down toward camp. Then the snag came loose, went airborne, and slammed ol' Tiny right in the butt.

My smile seemed to die somewhere between earth and my ultimate polar orbit. Tiny Man had had all he could stand. He bellered across a thousand hills like a wounded foghorn, and he swallowed his head and jumped forty feet in the air. I measured it later.

Down the hill we went. Tiny was bucking like he never had before in his life, that snag bouncing high off rocks and stumps and chasing Tiny down toward the lake. The experienced eastern High Sierra packer was trying to find something to hold onto.

It didn't work.

When it was all over, when the dallies came off the saddle horn and Tiny Man quit bucking, fifty yards the other side of camp, there were three things in a perfect line down that hill. First there was my hat. Then there were my glasses. Then there was me.

Tiny was kind enough to deposit me directly in front of my teenage dream girl in the middle of camp. I came to rest in a less-than-dignified pile of skinny packer, kinda stacked here and there in a painful mess. There was a rock on the landing strip somewhere. On cold days I can still feel it.

She looked at me in alarm, but then when I moved and got my eyes uncrossed, she said, "Is that really how the old-timers did it?"

She didn't mention anything about having my children, either.

The Ballad of Nimrod Bodfish

There's something about the size of this country . . . the vastness of it, the distances between places. And the weather, the weather that closes in and slams you down when you least expect it.

I guess that's why so many strange things happen in Alaska. People seem to be strangers here, always strangers. In order to live here, we can't do things the way people do Outside. We have to work harder to make it here, and we have to be very clever, because if we wait until we're in trouble, we could be real dead.

One of the strangest guys to come along in the history of this state was an old prospector and trapper who called himself Nimrod Bodfish. Gave himself the name Nimrod after the mighty hunter of the Bible, you know. He lived so far out in the bush that they had to import trees just so the forest wouldn't get lonely.

That cabin of his was up north, way up where the Yukon River widens out into a flat sea and curves its farthest north. Nimrod liked it out there. He stayed out there with his handful of sled dogs and ran a little trapline for beaver. He didn't worry about going to town until after breakup each year, when the ice was completely gone from the river.

He was that kind of a guy. He didn't need to be entertained, except by the antics of the red squirrels and the black-capped chickadees. Didn't need much out there. Dog food and people food and enough firewood to keep the sting of the cold out of his small cabin.

Ol' Nimrod would've just disappeared into Alaska history, would've become just another eccentric uncle who went North and was never heard from again, except for what happened one long, cold winter.

And what happened that winter slapped Mr. Bodfish straight into the pages of legend among northerners.

So here's ol' Nimrod, all gathered in for the winter. His dogs are fed and happy and ready to hit the trapline when the snow gets deep enough. His firewood stack is almost as big as the cabin. Nimrod brought enough old outdoor magazines with him to keep him occupied during the long cold time.

But then one morning, he feels something funny in his mouth. It's a slight toothache. But, as toothaches will, it doesn't stay slight. It grows and gathers speed and strength until poor ol' Nimrod can't stand it anymore.

There isn't much a guy can do out there without a dentist, and these were the days before everyone had two-way radios. But Nimrod found a pair of pliers in a box in the corner and decided to take care of the problem himself.

He had to sterilize the pliers, of course, as he didn't want infection to set in where the aching tooth had been, so he dove into his supply of liquid anesthetic, which comes in fifths of a gallon, you know, and poured some over the pliers. This gave him another idea. If he were to anesthetize himself with some of that good stuff, pulling that tooth would hardly hurt at all!

So he began the slow but happy process of killing the pain. In fact, he killed the pain so thoroughly that his hands weren't all that steady, or his mind that sharp, when he began his foray into the wonderful world of dentistry.

But he knew he had to get that tooth out, so he just got tough and pulled it out.

Strangely, though, the pain didn't go away. It turned out he had pulled the wrong tooth. So he medicated himself some more to cauterize the gap and attacked the next tooth.

Well, the medicating and cauterizing and extracting continued for a long winter's night. And when Nimrod woke up with an Olympic-class hangover, he discovered he had no more toothache!

He also discovered he had no more teeth!

Yep, he'd pulled every last tooth he had left in his head, but it left him toothache free and smooth-mouthed.

This presented a real problem, you see, because this was only the beginning of winter, and most of Nimrod's food required teeth to eat it, and he was fresh out of chompers. So our old sourdough pal was forced to ignore the beautiful haunch of moose hanging outside and content himself with oatmeal.

Oatmeal isn't so bad if you just kinda ease into it every now and then in the morning, but for a steady diet, it lacks a lot.

But Nimrod wasn't one to complain. He gummed his oatmeal. He ran his trapline. And he waited for the sun to return in spring. Oh, did he ever wait for that sun to return!

And when the sun finally came back to the land, something wonderful happened.

He was awakened one morning by his sled dogs carrying on something fierce. He looked out the window and there was a black bear in the yard trying to steal food from one of the dogs. Nimrod took the rifle down and shot the bear. When black bears first come out of hibernation in spring they taste awfully good, too. Nimrod hadn't had bear roast in a long time. But then, he hadn't had meat in a long time, either. And standing there looking down at that dead bear gave him an idea.

He carved some spruce into just the right shape, and then he pulled the bear's teeth and embedded them in the spruce with spruce pitch for cement. It took days of careful labor, but when he was finished, he had made himself a passable set of dentures out of the black bear's teeth.

The world then began to take on a rosy hue, and his diet grew to normal proportions. The sun returned and Nimrod went to town to buy supplies, and that caused some interesting comments, because Nimrod's smile kinda looked like that of a vampire because of those bear incisors. He could frighten children in Fairbanks half a block down the street. The word spread over the next few years about ol' Nimrod and his dentures, and one dentist who was vacationing in Alaska offered him a new set of dentures in exchange for the bear teeth. Nimrod jumped on that chance, and his smile returned to non-frightening status, and the dentist donated the bear choppers to his dental college's museum of curiosities.

Thus ended one of the strangest stories that ever came out of the bush. But for years, ol' Nimrod Bodfish claimed to be the only man to ever eat a bear with its own teeth, and I never heard anyone argue with that.

Night Ride
Fiction

———————————————————————————▶

The magic crescendo of day's end took forever to come, but it finally happened. The packer could look up to the west, above the tired ranch house, above the shady, whispering black locust trees along the alfalfa fields, and see the peaks of the eastern Sierra transform.

From the hazy-hot mountain range of the summer day, the peaks now became vertical battlements backlit by a setting sun. Each snowfield seemed larger at this time of day. Each peak strained upward through the sun blasts as if to declare their sovereignty before night cloaked them in mystery.

And the packer saw, as well, the blazing Inyo Mountains to the east, lit with the burnishing brush of evening, the rock spire of the Paiutes' sacred Winnedumah now absorbed by the mountains.

"Chores done?" It was the boss.

He nodded.

"Can't eat the scenery," the boss said, chuckling. "Get some food. Time to go." It was already getting dark when he began the saddling. Five horses, six mules. He tied the stirrups over the saddle seats with the saddle strings on the horses and checked each animal for shoes. Then he strung them together, being careful to get the right order.

You led the horses and tied the mules on behind. If you had trouble with the stock, it would come from the horses, not the mules. You led first the slowest horse, then the ones who caused you trouble, then the good horses, then the slowest mules, then the faster mules. Each collection of stock required some thinking before it became a functioning pack string.

"Lead ol' Jim," the boss said, unnecessarily. "He's the slowest. Always lead the slowest."

The packer nodded and ran lead ropes through the stirrups hanging on the near side of the saddles, and then tied large bowlines around the necks of the next animals. Six mules first, then the mules to the horses and finally to ol' Jim. One by one in the alkali dust and salt grass smell of the big corral until there were eleven head in one long string and ol' Jim's lead rope was dallied to the horn of his own rough-out saddle sitting on Brownie.

It was going to be another of those nights. Another of those special nights, he knew. Another gem in the necklace of a life he hoped would become heavy with such treasure.

He realized he wasn't talking tonight, except for a few words to each animal in the string as he worked on them. It made him smile, because the packer was naturally talkative, but talk could only profane a night like this, and he needed this night to be pure. Being silent was this mule packer's attempt at religious sacrifice. He would never say anything about it to the boss or the other guys in the bunkhouse, though. If any of them had similar thoughts, they wouldn't talk about them. There is an unspoken holiness in silence.

He tied his jacket behind the cantle, despite the sweaty hot evening and its brassy taste. He knew the winds coming off Kearsarge would bite deeply before he reached the pack station up there in that blackening canyon at 9,200 feet above sea level.

The boss stopped traffic on the highway as the packer rode Brownie and led the jittery, trotting string of animals across the pavement and up the start of the dirt road, then through the sage toward the night fastness above him. And then it was quiet but for the footfalls of the horses and mules as they once again figured where their places were and what their speed should be and turned from a herd of tied-together animals into a pack string.

As the road became a trail, and the trail went up into the mountains, the packer could look back at the ranch lights at the fort, and then look the two miles farther down the valley along the moving pearl string of headlights to the town lights of Independence, his adopted home. It's strange how those lights mean so much, huddled together in the face of such awe, gathering as if for company and support against the overwhelming mountains and the secrets of the night. He became aware of the moon only gradually, as he realized an hour later that he could make out Brownie's ears before him. Then he turned back to see each silvery animal work the slow switchbacks in turn, and he paused each animal length ahead of them to let them make the corners. There is a thrill and a pride in handling a really long string of stock, he thought. During the days in the high country, he seldom had more than five or six head behind him. But a man who can handle a pack train this long has reached the elite status of packer in this eastern rugged tall-nasty High Sierra country of California. A string like this one, on a moonlit night, alone, can earn a packer a doctorate in this unique craft.

During each of the summer days, he led the mules and took the dudes over the rocky, wind-snapped passes to the fishing lakes. He chatted with the people, reset errant horse- and mule shoes, enjoyed the scenery. But these night rides were special. The boss's stock truck could climb the switch-backed dirt road to the pack station in the meadow they called Onion Valley, but not if it had any stock in it. So on the days when some of the stock wasn't needed for the high trails, they were taken down to the ranch in the stock truck where grazing was a lot cheaper than feeding alfalfa. And when the time came to go back to the mountains, the packer had to ride at night to return them "up the hill" for the next day's work.

This meant riding all day, riding all night, then riding all day again, but it didn't happen often and the packer didn't mind that much, really. There were things on the night ride, he knew, that somehow paid the ticket for the fatigue.

And it made him smile. The stock didn't seem to misbehave as much at night, either. Maybe they, too, sensed what he did, that this was somehow a privilege and not just another long, dusty trail up the mountain.

At Tubbs Springs, he tied the string to an oak and went down the string, one by one, checking cinches, whispering reassuring words, making certain no saddle pads had slipped. Four cinches needed tightening. Not bad. The percentage was getting smaller each trip, he thought, and he felt pleased.

Then he swung back aboard Brownie, picked up the lead rope to Jim and yelled "Mules!" and they obediently swung into line again and headed for the brushy saddle known locally as Tubbs Summit.

By this time, the moon turned the horses and mules silver with its magic. It gave the packer an unspoken pleasure to look back on a sinuous Sierra snake of eleven animals stretched in a flexible line nearly 150 feet long behind him. And he looked up, straight up on the peaks of Kearsarge where the snowfields always left behind shady patches of dirty white, up where the Inyo moon splashed them with a dream brush and made old secrets come to life.

"You've heard of the ghost of Kearsarge," the old man said. "Everyone knows about her." The packers at the table at the ranch looked at each other.

"What ghost?" one asked.

"Just the old lady," the man said, with laughter in his dark Paiute eyes. "She doesn't hurt nothing, you know. Just sings a little."

The evening was dark at the ranch, and the table lamp splashed shadows of the assembled weary cowboys on the kitchen walls as they sipped coffee. It was always good to hear the stories the old man told, coming over from his own small cabin here on the reservation.

"I never heard nothing about a ghost lady up Kearsarge," said the cook.

"That's what they say," said the old man. "Ever since there was a town up there. Used to be the mine up there, you know. Big one. Then there was a big dance in town one Christmas time, it was. Long time ago. Before my time."

"Anyway, everybody went to Independence to dance, you know, except the caretaker and his wife. Avalanche got 'em. They were the only ones. Everybody else went to the dance. Can't remember what year it was. That mine was working then, though."

Nobody spoke while the old man sipped some coffee. "You boys ever hear her up there at night? You can hear her. That's what they say, anyway. Avalanche took her head off, you know. Never did find it. They say she calls for her head at night when there's a moon."

"At Kearsarge?"

"Yeah, you know where those old foundations are? That's where the little town used to be. Where the stock trail leaves the Onion Valley road. Looking for her head. That's what they say. Looking for her head."

The first foundations of Kearsarge glowed in the moonlight, little more than deliberate rock piles and scattered timbers now. The packer steered Brownie around the first and left the little stretch of dirt road again to follow the creek up the canyon. More foundations glowed, their old stones like age-worn teeth, and the wind came down from the snow patches cool and quiet. The packer thought he heard something, once. Just once, but he wondered about it, anyway. Maybe it was a night bird. Maybe. Looking back, the cluster of lights that was Independence had now shrunk to a small glowing nucleus in the moonscaped miles below.

He rested the stock on the first switchback above the old ghost town and pulled on his jacket. It helped.

"Your granddad told us there was a spook up at old Kearsarge," the packer said as they walked along the irrigation ditch that one night, a time back.

"Grandpa knows a lot," she said, squeezing his hand. "It's probably true."

He saw her eyes then, in the glow of a nearby streetlight there in town, as they walked. The desert night warmed them and made them both think of things long past and yet to come.

"You don't think he was just trying to b.s. us into being scared?"

"Not Grandpa. He knows a lot."

"Umm," the packer said.

"You like him?"

"Sure. Great guy."

"He likes you, too. He likes you a lot, I know. So do my mom and dad."

"Very nice people, your mom and dad."

She smiled up at him and he could see the pretty eyes again, the ageless eyes that spoke so much of generations of desert and mountain people, despite her youth.

"You like kids?" she asked.

The creek crashed down the mountain, heading for its igno-minious ending in the Los Angeles aqueduct far below. The packer took the rocky crossings slowly, stopping often. The longer the string, the slower he must go, until every part of this long silent snake had negotiated every obstacle smoothly. Brownie was used to the stop and go of the night rides with long strings and didn't argue.

And there was the magic, of course. The seductive sorcery of night in the place where the desert collides with mountains. It makes the longest nights shorter and the hardest rides easier.

He found the first of the pine trees at about 8,000 feet and listened once more to the breeze in the needles. And every now and then, in spite of himself, he listened for the voice of the lady without a head. Most of the horses were eager to get to the corrals and the hay, but the mules seemed content to look for moon-splashed grass clumps along the trail, clumps they may have missed on the last night ride.

The packer looked back each time the trail offered a view of the long string behind him.

The saddle horns on the horses and the forks of each pack-saddle seemed to be straight up. No animal was hanging back on its lead rope. No one had stepped over one. He could see this clearly, all the way back to the caboose mule. Sometimes he felt like the engineer on a train, except that each of his box-cars had a mind of its own.

Then, as the peaks surrounded them in moon shadow, the wind turned cold and the weariness hit. He pulled his hat down farther on his face, turned up his collar, and shamefully admit-ted to himself that he looked back less often. That's when he heard the lady. Just once. He was sure of it, but he'd never tell anyone. It was too private. Too special.

The moon was behind the crest of the Sierra as he rode Brownie into the blackness of the pack station yard. The boss was there to help him unsaddle.

"Everything go okay?"

"No problems," the packer said.

"By the way, happy birthday."

"That's right, isn't it. Thanks."

"How old are you now?"

The packer stopped to think for a second in his early morning weariness. Then nodded.

"Seventeen," the packer said.

REMEMBER, FOREST FIRES PREVENT BEARS!

→

Now that I think of it, not all strange tales are necessarily tragic or momentous or historic. Some are just . . . well, strange.

Let me tell you what happened one day back a long time ago to a mild-mannered small-town newspaper editor. He and his wife had started a small weekly newspaper which served a small village twelve miles from their cabin and a coverage area about the size of Arizona—but you could assemble all the people in that area in a good-sized Texas Baptist church.

We're talking bush Alaska here. Dog mushers, gold miners, a few hard drinkers, and the chronically overjoyed. In other words, a nice place to live.

Being a newspaper editor, even in a bush community, isn't usually that exciting, of course. It normally consists of finding out what's going on, what went on, and what will go on, and then putting as much of it in print as the law, and a sense of decency, will allow.

But this particular summer's day wasn't that normal. In the first place, it was going to be more than 90 degrees. Secondly, this was the appointed day each year when all the kids in the village got together to pick up trash. The little paper had certainly let everyone know about it, including where and when and bring some garbage bags and important things like that. And the paper also let the Big Secret slip, too: Smokey Bear would be there to oversee things and pose for photos with the young village cleaner-uppers. There was such excitement in the village among the under-twelve set. Smokey Bear! The symbol of the United States Forest Service! Everyone loves Smokey. At that time, it was the Bureau of Land Management boys who had the Smokey suit and would be up to celebrate the cleaning up of the little village of Talkeetna.

Did I mention it was hot? It was. Hot and dry. And it was hot and dry several hundred miles south of Talkeetna on the Kenai Peninsula, too. And, as sometimes happens, a forest fire broke out down there.

This required every single BLM'er to grab an ax and shovel and get busy, but it also left a pile of kids who would be disappointed if the only bear they weren't terrified of failed to appear.

The problem was easily solved, of course. The BLM guys dropped the Smokey Bear suit off at the cabin of the newspaper editor and told him he was it.

Hey, thought the editor, why not? It would be fun. After all, he loved Smokey, too, and it would be a grand thing to help ol' Smoke greet the kids.

Right.

So the editor, his wife, and their two-year-old daughter, Mandy, drove to the village. And while wife and youngster were helping pick up trash, editor went to a pal's cabin and changed into the Smokey suit.

Only then did he discover two of the three things wrong with the Smokey suit. The first discovery was that being inside Smokey's artificial brown fur was like wearing an insulated moose on his back, and the heat was stifling. The second discovery was that Smokey's eye holes were about six inches in front of the editor's eyeglasses, but were the size of an eyeball. This meant that he was able to see only about two six-inch squares of dirt about eight feet in front of him. To see anything else, he found he had to swing Smokey's head around, getting the lay of the land six square inches at a time. But what the heck. It's for the kids, right? Nothing's too much to ask. No sacrifice too great.

So the editor, deep inside the Smokey suit, slowly walked out of the cabin into the afternoon heat. It was slow going, walking just that fifty yards or so over to the village park where the kids were gathered in rapt anticipation of a visit by a national symbol. Slow walking. Not very good visibility, either. Oh, it wasn't just the six inches that was the problem, but the fact that wearing a fur coat during a heat spell causes perspiration, and the sweat ran down his face, streaking and soaking his glasses. Now this wouldn't have been too big a problem except that there was no way to wipe off the glasses, or even take the glasses off. So he just stumbled and sweated and walked slowly into Don Sheldon's hangar twice on the way over there.

Guided by the laughing and chatter of the children, he finally made it around Sheldon's hangar. He was on the home stretch now. Maybe twenty yards to go. Oh, inside that hot suit he was grinning. Hey, ol' Smokey will put in an appearance, pat the children on the heads for a job well done, and then he can go back to that cabin and dislodge a soggy editor, by this time soaking wet and blind.

Just before he reached the park, the editor discovered all at once the third problem with wearing a Smokey Bear suit. He was toddling along slowly when all at once there was a growl and the sound of racing paws, and then more growls and running, and then, as he stood there blind and dripping, wondering what was going on out there, he found out.

Smokey, of course, was a bear. Oh, he may stand upright and wear a ranger hat and have a belt buckle, but you can't fool Talkeetna dogs. They didn't spend all that time in the woods of Alaska for nothing. On the one hand, here's a park full of our precious children, on the other hand, attacking from behind Sheldon's hangar comes a . . . oh yes, baby, that there's a BEAR!

Kill Bear! Kill Bear!

Our pal Smokey then discovered that the thick fur suit didn't stop sled dog fangs from penetrating through fake fur. All of a sudden, arms and legs were punctured, dragged, pulled in different directions. There was fixin' to be a bear killin' and I mean, right NOW! And Smokey was the designated bear.

There just isn't a whole lot that a soggy blind editor can do about a dog attack while in that suit. In a brief second of recognition, he was even able to pick out the obese Labrador retriever whose job it was to hold down the rug in the Fairview Inn. That dog loved everyone.

But not bears.

On the heels of the dog attack came the attack of the children. Waving long sticks and whacking dogs as quickly as they could, the kids pummeled sled dogs until they backed up, all the time screaming "Don't hurt Smokey! Don't hurt Smokey!" The aim of the kids wasn't always that accurate, and Smokey himself was whacked pretty good here and there.

About that time, some compassionate adult took Smokey by the paw and led him, now dog free, into the midst of the children. Smokey put his paws around the happy youngsters and had his picture taken many times. He patted them on the heads for their efforts in the clean-up of the village. Then Smokey noticed his wife standing to one side, and she was holding their daughter in her arms. Hey, he had his picture taken with everyone else, why not with his own kid?

So he walked over and tried to take Mandy from his wife, and Mandy was one bush baby who shared the sled dogs' opinion of bears. She screamed to the world and Smokey was rebuffed by his own kid.

As an adult, the editor's kid, Amanda Randles, recalled the incident.

"I do remember the day. Vividly," she said. "The world was turned upside down, and my mommy was trying to get me to make nice with a bear. Seriously, I remember abject terror. It's one of those moments that burn into your brain."

Well, after everyone had his fill of Smokey, Smokey made it back to his pal's cabin and disgorged an editor who swore he was twenty pounds lighter than when he started out an hour earlier. The puncture wounds were cared for and the suit was returned almost intact to the BLM guys a few days later.

The editor never forgot that day, and has since looked with added respect whenever someone shows up in a Smokey suit. Was this story in the paper? Well, no, at least not all the inside information. But the editor that day was a guy named Slim, and it happened just that way.

Oh well, it's for the kids, you know. Anything for the kids.

Remember, only you. . . . Ah, you know.

STINKIN' SKUNK

→

H e has a brain about the size of a marble, can't see very well and isn't very fast. No, he isn't on the city council, but we all know him. In fact, we can be aware of him while driving sixty-five miles an hour down the freeway hours after his visit.

He's our striped skunk, the No. 1 animal we won't invite to a party. If points were given for unpopularity, he'd win the Nobel Prize. His smell can gag a sick dog off a gut truck, and that's before he sprays anything. The experts say Ol' Stripes can only spray up to fifteen feet. If that's true, how then can he empty a square city block with a single squirt?

He's not even popular in the animal family. The spotted skunk (who is no prize himself) doesn't claim kinship. Ol' Stripes is listed officially as Mephitis mephitis. Spotty clocks in as Spirogale putorius. The other varmint often associated with the striped skunk is the civet cat, which lives in Asia. But he's known in Latin circles as Civettictis civetta, which isn't even close to mephitis, either. Mephitis sounds a lot like Mephistopheles, doesn't it?

At least the civet cat contributes something to society. The Chinese eat him in a very popular soup. Not only that, but the civet cat contributes greatly to the rarest gourmet coffee in the world, Kopi Luwak coffee, which many people suspect of being a myth. This coffee comes from the island of Sumatra, where civet cats eat the coffee fruits and excrete the beans, which are then collected from the jungle floor and processed. The taste is reportedly much richer than typical coffee, with a chocolatey undertone.

Whoa now! You know, Mavis, I believe I'll skip the refill this morning. Running late for work as it is. This might just be a clue as to why this coffee is so rare.

No one claims Ol' Stripes for a relative these days. Maybe back when giant sloths hung around New Mexico, but if so, any cousins have since died of shame. Our striped skunk doesn't add a lot to our quality of life. Oh, as a plus, the ever-forgiving biologists point out that skunks eat grasshoppers.

Well, so do trout, and it's a lot more fun trying to get a trout to eat one. Besides grasshoppers, skunks enjoy canned sardines, peanut butter, and marshmallows. They carry rabies, stay out all night, live under the house, and smell bad. Had a cousin like that.

If skunks move under your house, they can be easily discouraged from returning by—get this!—using an unpleasant odor as a repellent. That's right. Roll a handful of mothballs under the house and the problem is solved. They can't stand the smell of naphthalene.

And, if worse comes to worst and Poochie should end up with a face full of skunk stink, forget the tomato juice. Here's a tip from Doc Minter up in the Jemez Mountains. Smear said mutt with a mixture of one quart of hydrogen peroxide, one teaspoon of liquid detergent, and a quarter cup of baking soda. Don't get it in his eyes.

Skunk stink can wilt saltine crackers when they're still sealed, evacuate neighbors faster than a forest fire, and topple Third World governments. You have to admire professionalism wherever you find it.

Ah, Mephitis, me lad! You may be gone from our sight, but the memory lingers on.

THE DANCING
MUKLUKS

⟶

Getting dark just now. Late, of course, because it's summer. See how those old spruces look like filigree against the sky? Always reminds me of Spanish lace. About my favorite time of day.

I remember a night just about like this when I heard a very strange story indeed. Little colder than this, though. Snow on the ground already, but it wasn't true winter. Just nippy enough to make that fire feel real welcome.

The other two guys had already rolled in for the night, I believe as much to keep warm as to go to sleep, and I was left up with another fella, an older gentleman. We were killing off the last of the coffee and just enjoying being there. Maybe it was the night or the coffee or just because I was friendly, I'll never know for sure, but he started talking to me about his early days up here in Alaska.

It seems he was a missionary priest here for years. He spent a number of years in one small Eskimo village over on the Bering Sea coast. Ever been there? Nastiest place in the world. Wind blows all the time, and there's nothing to get behind.

Now the way he told it to me, there were these three men who took a team of dogs and went out onto the sea ice to hunt for seals. You know how it is: you get fairly close to where the open water is, and there are these breathing holes the seals have every so often. Well, nobody thought anything of them going hunting, of course, but when they weren't back in a few days, their families became concerned. Several of the men in the village hooked up some dogs and went after them. They came back two days later with bad news. They found the team and the sled, but the men were gone. They could see where an ice floe had broken off clean and gone to sea, and the tracks of the men led right to where the break was.

Under the best of circumstances, a guy only has a few days of life in a situation like this, but these men were experts at this kind of thing, so there was hope.

When the rescue party returned, the wailing and the crying began.

An hour or so after their return, some members of the families of the missing men came to the priest and asked if they could borrow the basement of the church for a while. He said of course they could. It was the only building in the village with a basement, and it had an oil heater, and it was also just about the largest room in town.

The families of the men brought in some wet walrus hide and cut it into a long strand that reached diagonally across the room up near the ceiling. The priest said it was just like a clothesline. They kept a fire going real good in the furnace, and by morning that rawhide string was tight enough to twang, like a guitar.

After breakfast, the three families went into the church basement and hung three pairs of mukluks on that rawhide line. These were the house mukluks that are used for footwear at home. They just tied the laces together and hung them up. The priest couldn't make heads or tails of this, and it just got stranger the more he watched.

The families sat down beneath the mukluks and beat those walrus-skin drums and sang.

And the mukluks began to quiver. They actually danced a little bit on that rawhide line. All three pairs of mukluks danced and shook.

And the people kept singing. The priest didn't know what songs they were, because in those days priests weren't encouraged to learn the Native languages.

People from the village came and brought food with them for the singers. And people took turns with the drumming and the singing. Some singers would go home and sleep while others sang. And more people brought food. The singing was constant. It kept going day and night. And all this time, while the families sang and beat the skin drums, those mukluks danced on the line. Danced sometimes fast, sometimes slow, sometimes they just kinda swung back and forth. But they always moved, always moved. All three pairs.

One young pregnant woman, the wife of one of the men, stood against one of the walls and just stared at the mukluks. She looked as though it was her job to keep the walls in place. She wore a hand-carved walrus ivory necklace, and it rattled when she sang.

On the third day, one pair of mukluks stopped its vibrating, and several women screamed. The other two pairs of mukluks kept dancing. While the priest watched, the family whose missing loved one had owned the unmoving mukluks took down the mukluks, and crying, took them home.

This caused crying among the other two families, too, but they bravely kept singing and beating the drums. The young pregnant woman sat at the table now and sang, but she stared straight ahead and watched the faces of others who watched the mukluks. For some reason, she didn't want to look at them herself. Wouldn't you think that if two pairs of mukluks are vibrating, the third one would have to vibrate, too? This part just doesn't make any sense to me. Didn't make any sense to that priest, either.

Anyway, the next morning in the church, just before dawn, the priest heard screaming and ran down to the basement to see what was going on. A second pair of mukluks had stopped dancing, and the young pregnant woman was screaming and sobbing into the arms of an older man who might have been her father. After a few minutes watching the mukluks hang silently while the other pair moved, the family went into mourning and took the man's mukluks home.

This left one terrified family to sing and play the drums and watch the final pair of mukluks move in a quiet lonely little dance of life on that otherworldly clothesline in the church basement.

The next day, other people in the village spelled the family members and kept up the singing while those family members did their best to rest. But they couldn't rest. After only a couple of hours, the family members were back, and the singing continued.

And men from the village went again to the place where the ice broke away but found nothing.

The last pair of mukluks danced and danced and vibrated and shook, while the villagers watched for any signs of stopping. But there was no stopping. The mukluks kept going, day and night, for days on end.

After four days, the airplane landed near the village, the Coast Guard airplane, and the man whose mukluks danced in the church basement got out of the plane, to the great relief of his family. But he was the only passenger.

He went to the homes of the other two men and spoke with the families. Then he went into the basement to get his mukluks.

He told the priest and the villagers who were gathered there that the other two men died at precisely the time their mukluks stopped dancing in the church. The day after the second man died, he was picked up by a Coast Guard vessel and taken to safety.

Now why the priest told me that story, I'm not really sure. He must've guessed I wouldn't laugh at it. It's kinda hard to laugh at a true story. Well, I was a lot younger then, but even then I knew there are lots of things we don't understand.

But having mukluks dancing on a walrus-skin clothesline in a church basement ranks right up there on the list of things I still don't understand.

Riding to Hell with Captain Bob

➤

So blame it on me. Go ahead. How was I supposed to know how they do things in Michigan?

Where I live, rivers flow downhill rather than back and forth, and I had nothing to judge this by. But it was the exciting end to a perfect day in the Michigan woods, and that's a fact.

George Cornell and I had driven from his "swamp" near Lake City over to visit our mutual pal Bob Guenthardt and his wife, Sue, in Manistee. Bob had been something of a Manistee River–rat-type guy for years, and had guided fishermen there, but I didn't know that. All I knew was that he was an elk-hunting pard, he was tribal chairman at that time of the Little River Band of the Ottawa, and he knew how to have fun around there.

So we began the day in tree stands watching for whitetails, then we took Bob's boat up the Manistee River (back and forth, back and forth) fishing for steelhead, and finally Bob took me to a tree stand he had on an island in the river. I was to wait there, slaying any monster buck that came within my bow range. He took George to another tree stand downriver from me.

Well, there I was up a tree on an island, and I was having a wonderful time. The deer failed to materialize, as the weather had been a bit too warm for them to be moving much, but nothing could dampen the fun I was having.

I do recall hearing something going through my pack at the base of the tree, and I looked down to see a raccoon helping himself to my sandwich, but other than that, the evening was a study in orange light and black tree silhouettes. It was, to me, simply magic.

When it got to be completely dark, I heard Bob's outboard motor coming up the river (back and forth, back and forth) and he stopped at the base of the tree and called me. How he knew just where that tree was, I'll never know, because it was darker'n the inside of a cow's belly.

I hopped in the bow of his boat with my gear and he goosed the gas feed and we sped off into total darkness.

Allow me to repeat: *total darkness.*

Rummaging around in the pack, I found a flashlight and decided to help poor ol' Bob, who couldn't see a thing and was still driving this boat about thirty miles an hour down a winding river.

"Don't need it, Slim," he said, quietly.

VROOM! We careened around a bend in the river. Bob turned his flashlight on for one second, then turned it off again.

"I have better batteries than you do, Bob!" I yelled above the roar of the Evinrude. "I'll light the way!"

"No need. Just leave it off," he said.

Then the boat swerved around yet another switchback in that river and Bob turned his flashlight on for a second and turned it off.

"Don't you want me to help?" I yelled.

"No," he said, quietly.

I was a crouched in the bow of a maniac's boat being driven straight to hell at a hundred miles an hour. By this time I looked like a frozen hood ornament. You couldn't see anything.

"Aren't we going . . . you know . . . kinda fast, Bob?"

He laughed. "Relax, Slim. Everything's okay."

By looking straight up, I could sometimes see the tree limbs over our heads flying by like pickets on a fence.

"But, Bob . . . I mean. . . ."

"Slim," he told me, "I just turn that flashlight on when we make a turn so other people can see we're coming."

"But, Bob . . ."

After three lifetimes at light speed, with me aging ten years with every switchback in the river, we began to slow down. Bob finally throttled back and pulled the pitch-black boat over to the pitch-black bank of the pitch-black river and pointed up the rise to where the pitch-black pickup truck should be.

"Slim," he said, in quiet explanation, "I've been guiding fishermen on this river since I was ten."

"Oh . . . I see."

He laughed. "I'm going to get George now. Want to come along?"

"Well, you know, Bob, maybe I ought to stay here and kinda keep an eye on the truck."

Hey, how was I to know how they do it in Michigan? I survived. I just keep telling myself that. I survived.

A Little
Fishing Trip

→

It's not the where, or mountain air, that makes a
cabin home . . . it's the whom within the room.

—Slim Randles

Ambition, like the tides that suck at beaches around the world, must be taken at the right time. Taken, yea verily, and thoroughly shaken to its last furry clump until it no longer lies between an outdoor guy and fun.

Ambition is what I had that afternoon so long ago. And I was proud of myself.

We were building the cabin twelve miles up the tracks from beautiful downtown Talkeetna, Alaska. I'd like to report that the spruce trees for house logs were falling like blades of grass caught in a lawn mower to my very handy True Temper Hudson's Bay ax. But I can't.

Blessed by the same kind of timing as Lincoln's visit to Ford's Theater, we had chosen to build our humble log abode during one of the wettest summers in memory. What you do is chop down a spruce tree, lop off the branches, peel off all the bark, drag it to the cabin site, whack some notches in it for the corners, then find some way to lift it up on top of the others and drop it into place.

I was an expert at this, of course, because I had read several books on building a log cabin before moving to the bush. The books all agreed that a good day's work consisted of getting four logs up. Four? Heck, I could probably get four up in an hour! The writers of those books obviously didn't know about my ambition, you see.

But the rains kinda put a kink in the process. Truth of the matter is, when you peel a green spruce log, and it gets wet, it becomes covered with a slimy substance like wet soap. This makes it much easier to drop it upon yourself and smash limbs (yours) all to pulp.

So we chopped trees and waited for a sunny day to drag them in and put them up. If I recall, the sunny day was usually a Wednesday. So we camped out in two soggy tents and cooked over an open fire with wet wood. We called mosquitoes and no-see-ums and whitesox names that would make a dog musher blush, and generally had a wonderful summer.

Then we had friends up for the weekend. They got off the train and walked back in the woods to our campsite, and wanted to go catch the marvelous grayling and trout in Lane Creek, a two-mile jaunt up the tracks from our corral. At this point, with the walls up about three feet, the cabin looked more like a corral, you see.

So my wife, Pam, who never met a fish she didn't like, loaded up with fishing gear and turned the sled dogs loose and grabbed the rifle and off she went with our friends. But did I go along? Nay!

I had ambition.

The day was bright and sunny and I had logs to drag and work to do, and I couldn't sacrifice the kind of progress I could make on the cabin for a little fishing.

Even if that fishing on Lane Creek meant grayling fighting like tarpon, despite their small size. Even if that fishing meant watching a dry fly set down gently on the surface foam and watching it turn slowly until WHAM!

Not me. I was working. I was Man. *Cabin Builder Man!*

So I waved goodbye to them as they left, and rubbed my hands and started in on the cabin. I must have slaved for forty minutes before I realized that the sun was also shining on Lane Creek and the grayling in it, and that their army-green sides would sparkle like diamonds when they came flipping out of the water, and that was before I realized that dragging heavy logs around was turning out to be work.

Using all the words at my disposal, culled from years of study at two of California's finest junior colleges, I drew myself to full height and said, "The hell with it. I'm going fishing."

I armed myself with a fly rod and set off up the tracks after the rest of them. Now usually in that country, you carry a rifle whenever you go farther from home than the outhouse, and I've even had to use it once between the house and the outhouse.

But she had the rifle.

Or we take dogs along. They are the best bear medicine there is. Black bears are afraid of them and grizzlies eat them, giving you time to grab the rifle.

But she had the dogs, too.

So I was just happily whistling along up the tracks, armed with at least half a pound of fly rod and reel, a thoroughly dangerous man.

Between the cabin and Lane Creek, the Alaska Railroad crawls along the very edge of the Susitna River. On your left is a very wide, fast, and cold river. On your right is a series of cuts in pretty steep hills that go dang near vertical.

Truth of the matter is, you're either on the tracks or in the river along most of these two miles. So it was disconcerting to me to hear a noise up the hill to my right and see a young black bear cub. Like any dumb kid, he was playing around in the weeds and wanting to be my buddy.

I don't have anything against bear cubs except they usually come with a mama, and this one sure did. She was up at the top of the cut looking down on our burgeoning friendship and making disapproving sounds that reminded me of a chainsaw with gout.

"Good afternoon, Mrs. Bear," I said, cheerfully, facing the hill with my back to the river. "Didn't it turn out to be a nice day?"

While this was going on, Junior was getting closer. He was doing his little cutting-horse-type boinks around on the hillside, wanting me to come up and play with him. I didn't have that in mind right then. I would occasionally glance over my shoulder to see if the Susitna River had parted, à la Moses, but no such luck.

"Now Mrs. Bear," I said, as she went into a low-headed crouch and started down the hill toward me, "you sure have a nice kid there. Go home, kid."

Junior bear looked at me with one of those cute little expressions that said, "Me and you are gonna wrassle, and then we'll play with trucks, and we'll be pals forever . . ."

And then your mama will eat what's left of me. Yeah, I know the drill.

About that time, mama let out a terrifying whoosh, which bears do by blowing all the air out of their lungs at once. It is the ultimate threat, especially when punctuated by popping their teeth.

The whoosh is also designed to test whether any humans in the neighborhood retain any used food in their alimentary canals and to remedy that situation forthwith.

She whooshed and popped, and I was fixing to see how well those swimming lessons in the third grade would stand me, when Junior detected a note of disapproval in Mama's tooth popping and looked up her way. She wasn't at all happy with his choice of friends.

He scurried up the hill to her and she whacked him with a paw and sent him crying pitifully over the ridge and out of my life.

When my legs once again worked, I finished the hike to Lane Creek.

The fishing was really good.

SOAKED IN
SUMMER

————————————————→

W hen the world is hot and my skin is fried, scratching from the constant dry, let the clouds boil up, boil up high. And then shade the earth with the darkening sky and bring the secrets and the smell of rain. The coolness and the blessed rain, again.

Our land is brown but blessed, stressed in the heat, the shiny heat of day. The slender green of rivers slides along, striving to continue, to feed its own along the banks, the banks where the dust rises. Rises, powdery clomp by clomp as we walk, walk the shady way.

And though the heat, the dryness of heat, pushes down our weary feet, we plod along. Ours is the blessing of challenge, to live, to thrive in the heat. To toil and sweat, to make the cold drink at day's end that much sweeter. Sweeter as it goes down, cooler as it falls, dropping the coolness inside us and forcing us to smile. That summer smile. We begin to grin and know, as shades of evening droop on the western hills, that we did it once again. We were measured and we did it. Did it with our hands, today. Did it in the heat, today. Did it when we were tired, today. We are here, we have worked, the bread is ours, the sweeter, the heavier for the toil, for the heat.

When the heat falls hard, on many days, unquenched by the dark of night, we ask, in quiet times, we ask. Bring us the clouds, the black-bellied clouds, the clouds that softly hold the heads of gods in their moistening grasp. The clouds, those big-bellied busters that hold the violence, the wind, the flashes, the noise. The clouds we wait for and pray for and look for on the western ridge. Let them come, with their silver tops and their bellies black as night and cool as forgiveness. The summer clouds, the clouds that define our culture, our art, our summer, our hot, heavy summer. The clouds, the rain, the respite from the toil. To soak the thirsty soil. Bring the listening to the tin roofs as the clouds beat a tattoo for us. Let the magic come and stay, stay for a while, at least for a while, and wet us down, all the way down. Fill our pores, smooth our skin, wash us free of dirt and sin, with the rain, the cleansing, blessing rain. Sink the water to the core of the earth and push it through the dust, making it heavy and loath to leave the ground.

Bring the smells, too, of life, and water, and the heat and the cooling and friends and dogs that are wet and happy. Waggily happy, stick-biting happy, rolling in temporary mud happy, laughing with tongues no longer parched.

When it's done, when it's over, when we've had our treasure and the clouds have gone to feed the plains, when it's over, please, a rainbow. An arch of treasure and triumph and farewell and pleasure until the passion of the heat brings us yet another day like this. Another day of clouds, of life, of rain, of supreme love and comfort, of one more treat for man and his animal friends. Another day. Wait until it's right, but then, another day, please. Bring the big rollers in from the west, and let us watch the world get its fiery drink, and drink in the noise and think about cooler times, but know, let us know that there is nothing better than this.

A rain, a storm, a suddenness of life and blast and sweet charity designed to keep us living here, here in the rain, here in the sun, and keep us praying, here in the rain, and looking toward the west for more, always to the west, always looking for more.

THE STORY OF THE
GOVERNOR JAY

J ay Hammond was a very impressive man, whether you
knew him only as governor of Alaska, or personally, and
I was privileged to know him a lot as governor and some
personally. This is because Alaska is the world's largest small
town and I was a newspaper reporter.

But I didn't have a chance to visit with Jay on a personal
level until after I'd left the state. I was back up there on what
newspapermen call a junket, that is, a freebie trip for out-of-
state journalists. At the time, the summer of 1979, I was associate editor of *Petersen's Hunting Magazine* in Los Angeles, and
when the publisher asked if I wanted to go back to Alaska
on a freebie and catch fish and hug my daughter and other
pleasures, I told him without any hesitation I believed I could
squeeze it into my schedule.

We were wined and dined the length and breadth of the
Great Land, from Ketchikan to Prudhoe Bay, and I got to hug
my little girl, so everything was worthwhile. We were even flown
into Wien Airlines' fishing camp on the Alaska Peninsula, a
marvelous place where Noel and Sig Wien could entertain
customers and employees. There were so many brown bears in
that area that the entire camp was surrounded by an electric
fence to keep them out of the buildings. In this hilly but treeless

paradise, we caught six- and seven-pound rainbows every cast. After about half an hour of that, I tired of it, believe it or not, and spent the rest of the afternoon taking pictures of the other guys with their cameras.

But before leaving Alaska, we went to the governor's mansion in Juneau and had lunch with Governor Jay Hammond and Attorney General Av Gross.

Jay wasn't your typical politician, but he may have epitomized Alaskans in many ways. He was from the tiny Native village of South Naknek, was married to a Native woman, wore a beard, was a commercial fisherman, and was also a hunting guide and a bush pilot. In other words, he was everything all the rest of us wanted to be, and he did it all quite well.

So at lunch that day, with a table full of outdoor writers from around the country, Jay Hammond was in his element. And he told us his favorite grayling fishing story.

He had been flying around one day when a weather system caught him and forced him to land on a remote lake in his float plane. It was obvious he would have to spend the night there and wait for better weather before he could go home, so he made himself as comfortable as he could and prepared for a long night ahead.

"But right at evening," Jay said, "the grayling started rising in that lake. I mean, they were rising like crazy. I looked around in the plane and found some survival fishing stuff, but no flies, and I really wanted a dry fly right then to catch a couple of those fish for dinner.

"I did find some bare hooks, but no feathers of any kind. These fish were going nuts, striking at anything, so I thought, hey, I'll just make up something crazy. So I took some thread from my red long johns and used it to tie a kinda fly. It wasn't pretty, but the fish didn't care. I stood on the floats and pitched the fly out there and I was catching one every cast. I kept a couple for dinner and turned the rest loose, but it sure was fun."

After lunch, we were saying goodbye, and as I shook Jay's hand, I asked him what the fly looked like.

"You have a card, Slim?"

I did, and gave him one. "I'll tie up a couple and send them to you."

I thanked him and left with the others. Sure, I thought. The governor of Alaska has nothing better to do than sit around the old mansion tying flies for Slim. Right.

About two weeks later I received a little box in L.A. with two small red dry flies in it, with a note from Jay Hammond telling me to enjoy them.

I call them the "Governor Jays," and while I've fished with copies of them—successfully, too—those two will never get wet.

DEAR OL' BOONE

$\longrightarrow$

O l' Boone came into our lives right at the end of his, but although his bear hunting days were nearly done, and he acted more or less as an advisor to our other hounds, I wouldn't have missed having him in our family for anything.

Boone was a quite large Walker hound, maybe seventy-five pounds, and was something of a legend in New Mexico. He had been owned for almost all his life by a friend of mine who treed more than 500 bears with Boone. But then Boone got old and my friend gave him to someone who, it turned out, shouldn't have had him.

I was driving by Boone's new owner's place one day and saw the dog chained up short to the fence in back. I drove in the driveway.

"Say," I said, "isn't that Boone?"

"Sure is," this guy said.

The old dog couldn't even reach his water dish.

"He's yours now?"

"Sure is."

"Are you a betting man?"

"What do you mean?" he asked me.

"I'll bet you a hundred dollars you won't put Boone there in the back of my pickup."

He won the bet and I got Boone. My daughter Bridget and I just loved the old guy. For a hound dog man and out-fitter (which I was at that time) to have Boone in the yard was an honor. There are times when it's just wonderful to be able to spend money and feed a dog like this. He was a genuine celebrity. But lest the reader think this is a one-way homage to a great dog, let's dispel that right away. Boone (he was about fifteen years old at the time) gave as good as he got.

He had a positive attitude, a loving heart, and a sense of the ridiculous, which made him fit right in with our little bunch of mostly bluetick hounds. He was honorary uncle and grand-father to any puppies who happened to be around and delighted in babysitting them. And when you took the hounds to the mountains, he naturally had special privileges. When the other dogs were staked to trees, Boone lived in the tent with us. Age and reputation do have their privileges, of course, and he was there in the tent for any little snacks that we might have left over, and the only price we had to pay for letting him live like this was tolerating his snoring and passing of gas.

When we first got Boone, he was pretty stove up. He was no longer able to leap into the back of a pickup by himself. He was nearly blind, almost deaf, and could walk around for about five minutes before having to have a nap.

This led to learning one of his little tricks. I had to scoop him up in my arms like a large spotted sheep and put him in the back of the pickup, then lead him forward to where his snap was, just behind the driver's door in the pickup bed. And while I was snapping him, I noticed a certain warmth on my shirt. Ol' Boone, with a mischievous grin, had lifted his leg and was happily filling my shirt pocket as I fastened him. After the second time this happened (sometimes I can be a slow learner) I was discussing the dilemma with Doc Minter, my very close friend, hunting companion (Doc guided hunters for me for several years), fly fishing wizard, and veterinarian. Doc suggested I try some Comfort powder on the old dog.

Comfort is the brand name, vets call it S.O.D. (generically), and I don't hesitate in recommending it to any stove-up old dog that needs it. It works on most of them, Doc says, but not all. It worked like a champ on Boone.

It's this brown powder you sprinkle on his food. A vet has to get it for you, and it's expensive, about $35 at that time for a margarine-tub-sized container of the stuff. I'd use it again in a heartbeat, too.

After about five days on Comfort, Boone was able to jump in the pickup truck on his own. Two weeks later, he was hunting with the younger dogs. He'd get out of the truck, confirm that yes, this was a bear track, and get the boys started on the trail. Then he'd come back to the truck and we'd have coffee together. Well, at least I would . . . oh, you know what I mean.

Michael Candelaria and I took Ol' Boone with us on a memorable bear hunt to the Capitan Mountains (original home of Smokey, our national forest fire symbol) and on hunts in the Gila and the Jemez Mountains. But it was one night in the Jemez Mountains on a coon hunt that will stick in my mind forever.

I was up along Paliza Creek with my pal Chris Gleason and four or five of our dogs, including Boone. My Molly started a track out of the back of the truck, and we stopped and turned the dogs out.

It's about here that we need to point something out. Doc's magic powder got Ol' Boone's running gear working again in pretty good fashion for an antique pooch, but it couldn't really do much for his other problems. He still ran into things, like trees and mountains, because of his failing eyesight. He couldn't hear much of anything at all, and there was one other little foible. Ol' Boone's thinking processes weren't what they used to be. Oh, he'd still run a track, but wasn't really sure why. And that old hound know-how that tells a dog which way the animal was going, just by the smell, had pretty much failed him altogether. Now he was still broke straight, though. He wouldn't run a coyote or skunk or porcupine or deer. If Boone said it was a lion or a coon or a bear, you could take that to the bank. So we got to where we'd use him as a "check dog." Someone with a younger nose would sing out that she had found a track, and we'd turn Ol' Boone out. He'd toddle up there and sing out, "Yep! It's a coon! Real coon. Sure enough! Co-o-o-o-o-on here!"

Then we'd turn the other hounds out and they'd take it from there.

So this one night in the Jemez, along Paliza Creek, Molly sang out, Boone came out and said, "Lion here! Got us a cat! Baby, it's a bi-i-i-i-g cat!"

So the others came tumbling out of the dog box and took this lion's trail (I tried to get this big cat for several years unsuccessfully, I might add), ran it straight to the base of Roger Mesa nearby, and started straight up the mesa's vertical sides.

Chris Gleason is one of these people who can't sit still. In the rare times when he's between jobs, he works for free, because he has to work. And going hunting with his hounds and mine is no different. None of this sit-in-the-pickup,-sip-coffee-and-listen-to-the-music-of-the-night stuff for Chris. In case I haven't mentioned it before, he's about twenty-five years younger than me, too. This could be a factor.

And he's from Massachusetts, so he talks funny, too. He used to tell me about the rotten gun club back home, until I figured out he was talking about the Rod and Gun Club.

But he's a go-getter. So when the dogs went straight up Roger Mesa, Chris had to go, too. I didn't have to go. For one thing, I've been to the top of Roger Mesa, around by the other side where the trail goes up, and I've seen the view from up there, which is really nice, but only when the sun is shining. For another thing, I knew the last twenty feet to the top of the mesa were straight-up slickrock that no hound was going to be able to ascend, but was duck soup for a cougar with hounds on his butt.

So while Chris was scrabbling around arming himself with flashlights and things for his vertical trek, I relaxed in the truck. Why? Two very good reasons: 1. I'm about twenty-five years older than Chris (did I mention that?) and 2. Ol' Boone was still working the creek just outside the truck.

Dear Ol' Boone. If I hadn't loved the old boy for all the other stuff he had done, that night on Paliza Creek when his Canine Alzheimer's saved this oldster from a steep climb would have endeared him to me forever. Boone was in the creek, wading upstream for about 200 yards, then turning and bawling some more and working downstream for 200 yards, and then he'd turn and go upstream again.

"I'd better get after those hounds," Chris said, mentally in the starting blocks already.

"Good idea," I said. Now I figured they'd probably lose that lion at the crest of the mesa and come back to the truck, but I also knew Chris and that he wouldn't be happy without a midnight mountain ascent. "I think I'd better stay here and keep an eye on Ol' Boone."

"Good idea," Chris said, taking off into the brush.

An hour later, all I knew about Chris and the hounds was a distant bawling high on a black mesa, and the tiny beam of Chris's flashlight as he scrambled up in the rocks. But of course, I had much more important things to do. I had Boone, the wonder dog, down along the creek with me. No way was I going to let such a valuable animal chase whatever this up-and-down-the-crick varmint was by himself. He might catch cold or something. So I was forced to sit in the cab of the truck while Boone learned every pebble in that 200-yard stretch of creek. Yes, I had to sit there doing nothing but sipping coffee and listening to country music, while Chris had all the fun of climbing Roger Mesa and losing a mountain lion.

Finally, when the flashlight beam reached nearly to where I figured the top of this 1,000-foot vertical climb was, it turned and started back to the truck, and those hounds fell silent. All except Boone, of course. Dear Ol' Boone was still trying to figure out what had gone up and down that damn crick and what it was that had kept him busy sniffing and bawling for two hours.

When an exhausted Chris and the young dogs returned and collapsed into the truck, I went out and caught Boone as he went by and loaded him in the truck, too. He grinned at me. I grinned back.

I sure loved that old dog. Especially that night.

It wasn't much longer after that that Ol' Boone kinda disintegrated. He couldn't do much at all any more. He could just toddle over to the kennel gate and happily go BOOF! before his legs gave out and he had to take a nap. He couldn't see anything any more. He had to find the food dish by scent alone, and about the only thing that worked right on him was his tail. It still wagged.

Doc came by to check on him and I asked if it were time for The Needle.

"Well," Doc said. "He's sure suffering from Old Pooch, but he's not in any pain and wags his tail. If he doesn't eat any more or gets worse, call me, but I'd just leave him alone for now and see what happens."

So we did. And about a week later, I discovered that Boone had curled up for a nap in his dog house and hadn't awakened.

We buried him in the puppy pen. He sure loved being around those pups.

MOVING
THE HUNT

---►

B
y and large, the most wonderful part of being a hunting
guide is getting to know the hunters. Spend a couple of
weeks with a guy in inclement weather, suffer through
long hikes and disappointment with him, and then share the
wonderment of success with him, and you've made a lifelong
friend, even if fate doesn't let you see each other again.

These tend to be some of the world's nicest people. When
they come to hunt, they want to know the names of all the
little plants, and which berries are good to eat, and they want
to hear stories of other hunts. They soak it up. If they man-
age to take an animal or two or three, so much the better, but
they're having a great hunt anyway.

But that isn't always the case. On rare occasions, you'll run
across someone who just can't seem to enjoy himself no matter what happens. Such a hunter was a guy we'll call Don, an
architect from Houston, Texas.

Don was supposed to be having an unguided hunt for
moose, with the outfitter flying him in to a camp and then
flying him out later. This was how Don could collect a moose
in the cheapest possible fashion. But as fate would have it, the
outfitter was killed, and Don decided to take advantage of the
situation and demand a fully guided hunt from the outfitter's

widow. She asked me if I'd take him out for moose, as he seemed to be on the verge of suing if he didn't get his way. He made these demands on the widow, mind you, when the outfitter's body was still in the wreckage of the plane.

As I said, this guy was a real piece of work, the only one like this I've known in thirty years of guiding hunters.

I agreed, of course, and the next morning (before the boss's body had even been recovered) I set out with Don to find him a moose. As the morning progressed, I learned that Don really couldn't stand Alaska, because it rained all the time, and he couldn't get warm. Just that cold, cold rain, and how did we stand it?

"Don," I told him, "when I was in second grade in C. Russell Wilkerson Elementary School in El Monte, California, I knew Alaska was famous for having crummy weather. Why does this surprise you?"

He didn't think that was funny. What was worse, he didn't think I was funny. Some transgressions border on the unforgivable.

We walked some more along a ridge, and he started griping about guns. You always have to clean them. They're very expensive, and before you go on a hunt you have to go to the range and sight them in. They're just a lot of bother, and besides, the noise hurts his ears.

We got down in the thickets along Devil's Creek, and he started in again. This time it was moose. Moose were these very smart, very elusive creatures who kept hiding in the trees (which were as big around as my arm), and they were almost impossible to find. And then, if he killed one, he'd have to cut it open or something. He just didn't see the need to get so messy, and for what? So you could say you saved the meat like it says in the rule book.

That did it.

"Don," I said, "let's sit down for a minute, OK?"

I tried explaining to him that the only thing dumber than a moose was a flat brown rock, that they were roughly the size of courthouses—you couldn't hide one in a city—and that they were delicious.

He wasn't buying that. He still thought hunting was a joke and hunters were fools.

I looked at him carefully for a minute.

"So Don, why did you spend a lot of money and come up here where the weather's crummy and chase moose, which you don't like, with a rifle that you don't like, so you can cut one up, which you don't like? I'm a bit confused here."

He looked at me and brightened up. "It's all part of my seven-year plan, Slim."

"Your seven-year plan?"

"Yes. I plan to be a millionaire by the time I'm thirty-five, you see. And I need a moose."

I must have looked a bit perplexed, because he launched right into it.

"Back in Houston," he said, "I noticed that really successful people had animals mounted in their waiting rooms. I'm an architect, but I didn't have any animals, so I decided to come get a moose. I figured anyone could get a deer, because Texas is full of them, but to get a moose, you'd have to be well-off and could afford a hunt in Alaska."

He grinned and nodded his head, like this should clear it all up for me. It fell short, so he continued.

"What I figure," he said, "is to get a moose and hang it up in my waiting room. People will see it, think I'm successful, and bring me business. If I get a different animal each year, in seven years I'll be making more than a million a year. I worked it all out on paper."

"Okay," I said. "Let me see if I have this right. You don't enjoy this at all, and are just doing it so people will think you're successful and will make you rich?"

"That's it," he said, grinning.

I've never, before or since, had any conversation that came close to this one. I thought it was time to trot out the facetious card and see if it worked.

"Don," I said, "you're doing it all wrong. You're wasting time and money and making yourself miserable in the rain and you don't have to do it this way."

"Really?"

"You never heard of Jonas Brothers? They're this firm of taxidermists down in Denver. Hells bells, man, you don't have to get dirty and cold and shoot all those animals. No way. Just go talk to Jonas Brothers. From time to time they get mounts that people don't pick up and they sell them to the public. Let some other poor slob go to Africa and fight tsetse flies and get diarrhea and have all those shots and stuff. You just go see Jonas Brothers and buy some of that stuff already mounted. You can make up any damn fool story you want about how you stalked it through the steaming jungles and all that."

Now I swear this; he got a piece of paper and pencil out of his jacket pocket and wrote down "Jonas Brothers, Denver."

And he thanked me profusely. The next day he changed his plane reservations to stop at Denver on the way home, too. He left camp four days early and didn't get a moose that trip. But I'll be willing to bet his hunting trips to Denver produced a lot better results.

SMOKEY, SCOURGE OF SLED DOGS

►

We got Smokey when dear old Mama Cat died. Mama had been Pam's cat down in San Francisco, and Pam brought her along to Alaska. When we moved to the bush, Mama went with us. When we built a cabin, she was the first to move in.

When she finally died of old age, we got another cat immediately. This was not so much because we missed the companionship (although we did) but because in Alaska's remote cabins, a cat keeps the shrews away. If you have a cat, you won't even see a shrew or realize they exist. If you don't have a cat, you have to stay awake at night keeping them from carrying you off to some remote cave and eating you alive.

They are about the size of a thumbnail, and if they were as big as hamsters, we'd all live in trees.

So we finally found a kitten—well, a half-grown cat, actually—down in Palmer on a farm in the Matanuska Valley. This was a feral barn cat they had live-trapped, and we drove her back to Talkeetna in the car, then put her in a pillow case and put her on the sled for the twelve-mile trip up the tracks to our home. She wasn't a happy camper during the car ride, and told everyone how miserable she was, but when we stuck her in the sled basket, with five big dogs pulling the sled, she had sense enough to ride quietly to our home at Trinity Creeks.

She was a small cat, never weighing more than maybe seven pounds, soaking wet, pregnant, and with clumps of snow on her. And she was gunmetal gray, which gave her the name Smokey.

For three days, Smokey was a wild cat, living in fear behind the couch, coming out to eat and use the box only at night. Then she jumped in Pam's lap, and said, "Hi. My name is Smokey and I'm your cat. Pet me *now!*"

Just like that, the wildness was gone, and we had a very sweet loving cat. She was great for lap petting and purrs and all that good cat stuff. She was very sweet and loving to human beings, but that milk of loving kindness did not extend to the sled dogs.

She was smart enough to stay well out of chain-reach of the big dogs. They would subdivide a cat in no time, I'm afraid. But there were always the puppies.

Oh yes, the puppies!

These friendly little fluff balls would toddle around out in the timber, making friends with everything, pretending they were tough, playing the puppies' favorite yard game called bite-my-butt. Then they met Smokey.

There wasn't anything that little cat could do about the grown dogs, they were beyond her sphere of influence. But those pups? Dead meat.

Each, in turn, would toddle up to her to make friends and she'd stick the needles in those poor little boogers and send them screaming through the woods. One after another, she got them all. She'd wham bang on them until they thought they were going to die; then she'd leave them and stride away with her head held high in triumph. After a day or two, all Smokey had to do was walk out on the porch, and all puppy happiness stopped in mid frolic. They ran to their mother as hard as they could and cowered inside the dog house, while their mama guarded them as best she could while on the chain.

Well, old dogs die, and young pups grow to be seventy-five-pound sled dogs, and the seasons roll. In a couple of years, and after several litters of puppies, we witnessed an interesting phenomenon. Smokey would walk to the door and ask to be let out, and the minute she set foot outside you could hear Wham, Wham, Wham as huge sled dogs hit the back walls of their dog houses, lying quivering at the sight of her.

"She walks!" they seemed to whisper.

Sometimes, if a dog ventured too close to the chain limit, Smokey would look at the dog, fluff herself up to the dimensions of a ten-pound cat, and just hiss the bejesus out of that poor mutt. The trauma was too much for them.

One year we moved to a rented cabin on a road to the south of Talkeetna and started a little weekly newspaper called *The Susitna Valley Chronicle*. Those of us who published it knew it as *The Kitchen Table Miracle*, because somehow or other we were able to put a paper on the street each week.

But this cabin, too, was in the woods. On a road, but in the woods and a nice place to keep a dog team. By this time, nearly all our dogs had been thoroughly Smokied as pups and were terrified of her.

An interesting thing happened about this time. Somewhere in Alaska, Smokey had managed to trot off into the woods and find a full-fledged tom cat and had returned to the cabin with an expectancy of kittens. They were born under the house, by way of a crawl space, next to the oil furnace. Nice warm spot for them.

She loved those babies as much as she hated the dog team. She was a very good mother. Finally, they got big enough so Smokey could take a break from being a mama and come out to socialize now and then. One early spring day, with lots of snow still on the ground, Smokey and I were sitting on the front porch looking down the yard to the trees where the dogs were chained. Her kittens were safely under the house, with their access door around the corner from us, out of sight.

That's when Connie, a pretty Siberian, decided to have puppies. As we watched, she squatted and dropped a pup. This was her first litter. Leaving Smokey on the porch, I walked down, picked up the puppy from the snow, and stuck it in Connie's house. She went in and went to licking it. I unsnapped her then, so the chain wouldn't interfere with parturition, and left her to having her babies. Smokey and I watched her from the porch.

Connie cleaned that pup pretty well, then suddenly realized she wasn't chained any more. Oh happy day! The most wonderful event in a sled dog's life had just happened. Not the puppying, but being OFF THE CHAIN! To celebrate, she left the pup and went streaking off through the woods to celebrate her freedom. I got up to go catch her, but it wasn't really necessary, as she stopped, about forty yards into the trees, and had another pup. By this time, she knew what to do, so she picked up the pup in her mouth and trotted back toward the dog house.

None of this would have been noteworthy except for one thing: Connie had to walk past the crawl-space hole and past the porch to get to her dog house. When Connie walked past Smokey carrying something small and squeaking in her mouth, and she had just come from where Smokey's kittens were stashed, red lights and sirens kicked in. Assuming Connie had one of her kittens, Smokey made a twenty-foot leap off that porch and whittled an elaborate carving on that poor dog's butt. Connie was running as hard as she could to save her pup and herself, and Smokey was determined to subdivide a sled dog and retrieve her kitten.

That poor dog thought she'd been attacked by a chain saw.

I ran and grabbed the cat (and paid dearly for it, I might add), and let Connie go back in the dog house to continue her new hobby of motherhood. I was forced to take Smokey up, crawl under the house with her, and have her count each kitten before she was able to relax and commute the class-action death sentence she'd just passed on all dogs.

I'll bet to this day there are dogs and descendants of dogs who know the legend who hear the mewing of a cat somewhere and cringe, wondering if it could be the legendary Smokey: Scourge of Sled Dogs.

THE PAINLESS
CONVERSION OF
A NONBELIEVER

▶

Transformations are strange things. Sometimes they occur in a wild dream, sometimes in church, sometimes where you least expect it. And sometimes a life-changing transformation for an outdoorsman takes place in an outdoor church, a cathedral of rocks and rare air and light and sparkle and beauty. That's how it happened for me.

I don't pretend to compare an epiphany that switches a man from salmon eggs to dry flies with some people's life changes from drink to lives of self sacrifice, of course. But sometimes I wonder which epiphany is the most fun.

Before that afternoon at Cottonwood Lakes in the eastern High Sierra, I'd been a lackadaisical fisherman. You tied on a bait hook with a worm or salmon egg on it. Or, if you were at a lake and really craved action, you rigged the spinning outfit with a Super Duper or a Mepps Aglia and started tossing and cranking. Sometimes, if the planets were lined up and fish were desperate, you could get a little action and some trout to roll in cornmeal.

That's how it was for me. That's why I always preferred hunting to fishing, because at least hunting required some skill and education and practice in order to get close. Spin fishing and bait fishing were like going to Las Vegas and pulling the handles. If the fruit lined up correctly, you got a fish.

Then one afternoon at way-too-much above sea level, I met the golden trout of the high country. I had taken a party in to the lakes and camped them, and there was still plenty of time before dark, so I got out my takedown spinning outfit and plowed useless rows across the otherwise pristine surface of the lake. My party was a family, I remember, but I am embarrassed to say I can't remember their names. (But after nearly half a century, it would be something of a miracle if I could.) The father of the family put together a fly rod and then came to join me. He stood there watching me and encouraging me, and he kept looking at the sky. "Fished here before?" he asked.

I told him no, that in fact this was my first time to Cottonwood Lakes. It was south of our usual region. Sequoia-Kings Pack Trains usually just worked five outside passes, beginning with Shepherd's in the south, and continuing north through Kearsarge, Baxter, Sawmill, and Taboose. Taking a party into Cottonwood Lakes, down in the Lone Pine area, meant we were helping a pack outfit to the south who couldn't handle the load.

"Ever fished with a fly?" he asked. I shook my head.

"It's kinda fun. A lure like that on a golden trout is like shooting quail with a .30–06. Overkill. You might catch one, but why?"

He fired up that fly rod then and made some of those long, lazy, sinuous false casts and then laid a dry fly gently on the surface of the lake, barely causing a ripple.

He cast a few times without result, and I was thinking I was getting as many fish as he was. Zero. So why was fly-fishing any better? I must admit, however, that his casting was balletic and beautiful.

"They're not biting today," I said, as though I knew what I was talking about.

"Not yet," he said, looking again at the sky. "About five more minutes, I figure."

I looked at him kinda funny. He grinned. "I just like to get in a few casts for practice and for fun. It's just fun, you know."

"Five more minutes?"

He looked up. "About that."

He then explained that golden trout don't rise to feed in full sunshine, but that you have a pretty good shot at them once the sun either sets or goes behind a cloud. Well, there was a good-sized cloud heading for the sun, with about four minutes to go. Maybe three.

"Want to try fly fishing?" he asked.

I didn't want to handle his fly rod and maybe break it, because it looked really flimsy to me, but he assured me I could fly-fish with the outfit I had.

"Take that lure off and put a bubble on that line and let's get you rigged up."

So I took off the Super Duper and I put a plastic float on the line about six feet from the end, and he tied on some flimsy leader and a dry fly. If I remember correctly, it was a mosquito, about a size 16. And yes, I can remember *that* after nearly half a century.

Then the world settled down and a shadow came rushing to us down the rocky scree slopes and darkening the snow patches, and then it spread across the top of the lake. And the fish began rising. They came up to the surface to feed and dimple the mirror plane with their little jumps and grabs.

He cast a fly out there, and I saw it settle almost imperceptibly on the surface. WHAM! And a six-inch golden was his.

"Now you just cast out there," he said. "That float will give you the weight you need to cast. And when you've cast, just take up enough slack to straighten the line, and watch what happens to the fly."

So I did.

WHAM!

And another fly fisherman was born. We fished until the cloud passed, and waited and talked until the next cloud came along and the silence of the high lake was again disturbed by the minute splashes of feeding trout. Then we caught some more, and released a lot more than we kept, and I decided fishing could actually be fun. He showed me how to false cast with his rod, and how the weight was all in the fly line, and I actually kept from snagging anything and I caught a small trout with his rig, and discovered that a six-inch golden could feel like a real fish if you have a light enough fly outfit.

I remember something else, too, from all those many years ago. This man was fishing with a Fenwick glass fly rod, and I remember just how weightless that rod felt and how proud he was of it.

In the years between then and now, I've had glass fly rods, one steel fly rod, and a number of graphite fly rods. Some of them were fantastic, too. Others were more pedantic and ho-hum. But I remembered that Fenwick at Cottonwood Lakes, and I remembered how it felt.

And today I have two of them out in the garage.

DAVE'S BEAR
FICTION

———————————————————➤

The bear had experienced good years: beautiful summers and autumns when the living was easy and the winter sleep slipped in quietly and full.

Things had changed.

There is a desperation that comes on a grizzly bear with age. When a bear has won his battles, reproduced his strength with another, taken his share of game, the kindness Nature owes a completed job is a swift death. As he had taken his share of moose and caribou quickly and surely, the bear deserved to go as quickly as the whisper strike of the hunter's bullet, or the quick crush of a younger bear.

But now the bear was old, and age brought with it indignities that are unseemly to wild creatures. The teeth that had crushed the life from so many were now worn knobs. The split-second reflex of muscle that could have brought down the swiftest race horse had slacked to a lumbering shuffle through the snow. His silver-streaked hide, once shiny and rolling with muscle, now hung in dull folds over the remnant of his body. Food was hard to catch.

There hadn't been enough food this fall to allow the bear to go to ground. Within his brain ran two urgent thoughts. He was burning with the desire to eat and sleep, and that desire was contradicted by his passion to avoid the wolves. Asleep in a den, neither the bravest nor hungriest of wolves would dare dig him up. They could not tell from the outside of the den that this was an old bear. It was simply a bear. His scent and his wide track were the only signs now of his former majesty.

If wolves caught him in deep snow, he would be surrounded and nipped until his strength left. His tender parts would be eaten even before life had left his body. It was an indignity reserved for those who survived beyond their time.

So the bear shuffled along the windblown ridge where the snow was thinnest, following the only sensory organ left to him in full: his nose. Up ahead was blood. That it was blood from a ptarmigan sprinkled on a marten set, he couldn't know. Perhaps years ago that message would have penetrated to his hunting brain. But time had slowed the flow of information into the most basic parts. Where there was blood there was meat. Where there was meat, he must go. He must eat and then sleep.

And the bear shuffled along the ridge slowly, heading for Dave's trapline.

The first set on the ridge had a few interested tracks around it, but there were no takers. Dave looked long at the scene, and tried to reconstruct the happenings. Read the sign and see what went wrong, he told himself. Where did the marten first suspect this was a set? Right there. Then he circled around to this knob to take a closer look. Dave was proud of this ages-old trapper's skill, learned day by day by looking at the impressions of feet in snow and deciphering track by track what transpired.

But to get so close and not score was disheartening. It wasn't so much the money, Dave had to admit. The money from the fur would help, of course, but Dave was a cautious man, and had planned to spend the first winter simply learning to trap. It was more than that. It was the slap in the face the wary marten had given him. The animal, wearing his natural sable, had pranced within inches of the traps and scorned the best efforts of the trapper.

In the past weeks, Dave had learned more than trapping; he had learned the delicious anticipation felt by generations of trappers and prospectors. Snowshoeing through the forest was in itself a way of life, but when it coupled with the anticipation of rounding the next curve of trees, alert eyes searching for that first sign of fur, the frenzy of the animal's last minutes in the traps before it succumbed to the cold, that's what kept him going. It was the same with prospectors. That is why so many are content to simply locate the gold and let others do the work of mining it. It was the thrill of finding it, of working with and against Nature, of plotting his skills against those around him and winning.

The bear jumped him on the third trap.

There hadn't been warning enough to get out the pistol. There was just this crushing weight and the frenzied attack. He thrashed in the snow in the arctic gear, making futile attempts to fend off teeth. Each time he fought, the bear roared and bit. The first attack opened skin on Dave's face. The second laid the skin back over his eyes. He could no longer see clearly. It wasn't until the calm between the attacks when he heard the rumbling over him that he realized he was in the grip of a bear.

He had gotten between the bear and the dead ptarmigan, which was unforgivable. The bear looked down at the quivering hunk beneath his weight. Dave tried holding his breath. The pain of the torn flesh had not yet reached Dave's brain, and the natural instincts now emerged cautiously and told him to lie still.

It worked.

After a few more bites to Dave's shoulders, the old grizzly stepped off Dave's back, carefully picked up the dead ptarmigan and walked away.

It was minutes before Dave moved. He didn't feel the cold, but he began to feel the pain. He listened for the bear. There was silence for long minutes, then Dave heard the grunting down in the creek bed, and he tried to see.

The world was a crazy red. When he sat up the pain began. A moan escaped him, but he instantly silenced himself and swung his head to see whether the bear understood the sound.

Thinking methodically, he moved until he was certain no bones were broken, then pulled himself slowly erect by clinging to an alder. Feeling his way down the packed back trail, he shuffled step after step toward the cabin. It wasn't far. Just a lifetime. A lifetime of victory and defeat. He was alive, and he had been beaten by the world.

Through the red-pained haze he shuffled as the bear had shuffled, feeling his way along the packed trail, trying to close out the pain.

He knew he was home only by the frantic barking of Queenie, the slamming of the cabin door, and Melody's screams.

Dave was lying in his bed. He felt cold water on what was left of his face. Melody's eyes focused on the face before her, but her brain mercifully shut out the sight. She worked methodically to stop the major bleeding.

"The neighbors have a radio. I'll go call."

Dave shook his head.

"Bear . . ."

"I know, darling. But I must go. Don't move until I'm back. Promise me? *Dave! Promise me?*"

Dave nodded painfully, his thoughts jumbled and swimming and blurred.

He started to sit up, but Melody pushed him back down. He said, "Take Queenie."

Melody said she would, then dressed for the cold and left the cabin.

Dave tried everything to ignore the pain during those hours. He tried to will the pain away. He fought the pain, as if by doing so he could conquer it. He told himself that if there was pain, at least there was life. If life continues, the pain will be forced to stop eventually.

But the pain became heavier and heavier with the hours. It began with the face, but it soon spread to the shoulders where the heavier bites had been made. It roamed around his body like a snake looking for opportunities. It found bruises where the bear's weight and claws had done minor damage, and set up outposts in these places, adding to the total weight.

Thinking was becoming very difficult. Dave's premise that pain could be ignored was faulty, his faith that where there is life the pain must leave, wrong. There was still life, but the pain grew worse. It became like the air during a cold snap. It had a weight and a pressure and a substance of its own. It was like a cancerous growth, spreading rapidly, taking over his body, making him doubt the most deep-seated feelings of his being.

He opened his eyes to search for an answer to the pain. Through a red haze he searched, looking for a last opportunity to win the battle.

Through the unfocused haze, Dave saw the big rifle hanging over the door. He stared at it and tried to look through it. He tried to go over each of its actions and weigh the possibilities.

When he tried to reach it, the pain clubbed him into unconsciousness.

He awoke briefly as hands moved over him, and deft fingers probed his face. He later remembered only the whopping of the rotors as the helicopter lifted from the lake, but he knew the cool softness of Melody's hand on his during the flight.

OH BADGER
ME NOT . . .

---------------------------------------→

I first became a husband—or became a first husband—before
I was old enough to vote or drink. Sometimes things just
happen that way. But those couple of years sure had their
compensations.

My wife came from a farming family in a tiny mountain
valley in California. I was an animal husbandry major in college, and when I was at the farm I got to drive tractors and hunt
deer and all kinds of fun things. Besides, Monterey County is
one of the prettiest places in the world. In addition to those
privileges, I was blessed to discover, membership in the family
had other benefits. Like going coon hunting with Cousin Ted.

Cousin Ted lived up one of the side canyons near what was
known as The Old Home Place, which by then was just some
trees surrounding a blank space where a house once stood for
more than a hundred years. Ted lived in a mobile home near
there. He did various things during the day to pay expenses,
such as take old dead machines apart and pour oil on them
and himself, and I believe his wife had a job during that time.

But Cousin Ted was a hound dog man. He had dogs tied
to trees and dog houses all over the place. When I was first
on the farm, I thought it was kinda ridiculous to feed so many

dogs, never thinking that someday I would be as rabid a hound dog man as Ted was. When I met him, I just thought it was stupid. But being a member of the family automatically gave me coon-hunting privileges with Ted, and if anything had the word *hunting* in it, it was fine with me. I couldn't wait.

Finally, one winter night when all was crisp outside, here came Ted in the station wagon, the windows all fogged up by dog breath. I leapt in with my flashlight and off we went. I learned about the California hill country method of coon hunting that night, which meant spotlighting farm fields until coon eyes were seen, and then turning dogs loose.

We got several coons and were heading home, and I have to admit I was really taken by the night music of those dogs. It seemed to me we were part of something very old and very elegant and very earthy. Forty-five years later, I still feel the same way.

So we were cruising along near the Lewis Creek bridge, taking turns wiping the dog-breathed windows free enough to allow Ted to see, when we spotted something lumbering along in the road ahead.

"Whoa Baby!" yelled Ted, "Look at that, look at that!"

He slammed on the brakes, and a big Walker mama dog who had been drooling down the back of my neck came flying over the back of the front seat and dove between my legs to the floorboards. I suddenly had a face full of dog belly, and neither one of us was happy about that.

"Turn the dogs out!" Ted yelled, "But keep Roscoe in there!"

Roscoe, I'd been told, was the "kill dog." I wasn't sure what a kill dog was, but I later learned it was a dog with more guts and teeth than brains and sense.

Roscoe stayed in the car, and the other hounds went bawling off into the night for just a few minutes, and then the whole tenor of the bawling changed abruptly to what I later learned was a tree "chop."

"Whoo! Talk tooooo-oooo-em!" Ted yelled. "They're treed, oh wow, they're treed."

"What was that thing?" I asked.

"Badger!" said Ted.

"Do we want a badger?"

"Worse'n about anything!" he said. "And we got one! Oh wow, this is just GREAT!"

So we ran up the road a ways carrying our flashlights, and heard dogs bawling on either side of the road at a place where the road crossed an arroyo.

Ted went flying down off the road, with me right after him, and found dogs baying treed on each end of about a three-foot culvert pipe running under the ranch road. And just about halfway down that culvert pipe was a very unhappy badger.

"Well," said Ted, scratching his head, "we need to get that guy out of there, obviously. What do you think?"

With all the wisdom of my eighteen years and zero badger-hunting knowledge, I mumbled some agreement. "How do we do that, Ted?" I asked.

"Simplest thing ever," he said. "We smoke that son of a bitch out of there."

I'd read about that. In those hunting books. You smoked something out. Of course, I'd always pictured building a little fire, and putting grass on it to make it smoke more. Stuff like that.

"Okay," said Ted, pulling a cigar from his pocket and lighting it, "here's what we do. You get in there with this see-gar and just smoke that rat bastard right out the other end of that pipe."

"Are you sure that's how you do it, Ted?"

"How many badger hunts you been on, Slim?"

Properly chastised, I took cigar in mouth and flashlight in hand and got on my hands and knees and crawled into that culvert pipe. I had dogs giving me moral support, quite loudly, at each end. I got in a few shuffles' worth and the badger hissed at me.

"Ted," I said, "are you sure?"

"Smoke that sucker out of there, Slim! You're doing just fine."

So I puffed and puffed and tried to blow the smoke his way, and he blinked a time or two and hissed some more. He had teeth. I could see them just fine.

"He backed up a couple of steps, did you see that?" Ted said. "You're doing great. I'll go get Roscoe to help you."

So I puffed and coughed and waited for Roscoe's help, and I'd just about decided that this part of badger hunting was one I could do without.

And then here came Roscoe.

Roscoe was pure terror with teeth wrapped around it, and he came boiling in the other end of that culvert pipe, ran straight to that badger, and chomped right down on his butt. The war was on, and both of them were heading for me.

Ted didn't have a stopwatch with him, but he later guessed I'd set the world's record for backing out of a culvert pipe on my hands and knees that night. He said the glowing end of that cigar in my mouth looked like the exhaust on a jet fighter.

One of the problems about living in a remote mountain valley where nearly every neighbor is a shirttail relative is that there are no secrets. In this valley is one little business, a combination store, gas pump, and coffee bar known simply as "the station." A couple of days later I was sent to the station to get some things, and there were two old ranchers sipping coffee and solving the world's problems.

They saw me and whispered a little back and forth and smiled. "Hey son," one of them said, "aren't you the one they call Slim?"

I nodded.

"Is it true you tried to smoke out a badger with a cigar?"

Laughter can sometimes be cruel, too, you know.

My young beautiful wife told me that, since I belonged there now, I could go hunting with Cousin Ted any time I wanted to.

After the divorce. . . .

THE
WOLVERINE
PELT

————————————————————————▶

I t was the wonderful and mysterious John Ireland who introduced me to the Talkeetna Mountains method of harvesting wolverines.

John was our neighbor one winter when Pam and I babysat Stephan (pronounced Step-ANN) Lake Lodge in the middle of the Talkeetna Mountains. The lake is about seven miles long—it's fly-in only—and the lodge is on the western side of the lake. If you slogged through the muskeg, or ran down along a ridge to the south about seven miles, you'd come to a much smaller lake called Murder Lake. Yes, there was a famous murder there many years ago involving the local Indians headed up by Chief Wasilla Stephan.

The only resident of Murder Lake back when we were in the area (the winter of 1972–73) was John Ireland. He lived alone in a cabin on the lake, along with a leather-stitching machine the size of the Eiffel Tower. He had to have it flown in in pieces and then reassembled it in the cabin. John made some of the finest purses, knife sheaths, or just about anything else you could think of to make out of leather. He went to Anchorage three times a year to mail off his leatherwork and to pick up supplies.

The last time I saw him, he was trying to get it down to two trips a year because he couldn't sleep in town. To properly visualize John, picture a cross between Santa Claus and St. Francis of Assisi. He had a gray beard and a pet gray jay (known thereabouts as a "camp robber") that he'd nursed back to health. In the winter, a cow and calf moose lived in his yard for protection from wolves. He wouldn't even have a dog, as the dog might keep wildlife from feeling welcome at his place.

We saw John because of the radio. The radio would just drive him nuts. He had this souped-up battery radio down at the cabin, and he had run some antenna wire out of the cabin and up to the top of the nearest ridge, maybe a mile away, where he wrapped it around trees. After the sun went down, John could get Arcturus on that darn thing. But what he really wanted was to get pioneer talk-show host Ira Blue on KGO in San Francisco. Unfortunately, he got the program clear as a bell up there at the top of the world. So, after a frustrating night of listening to callers who didn't share his particular political views (and I don't even remember what they were, to tell the truth), John would strap on snowshoes and walk seven miles just to drink coffee and comment on "those idiots Outside" who called the show.

It was during one of these pressure-valve meetings over Pam's coffee and cobbler that John mentioned the wolverine.

"Ever seen the wolverine hanging on the wall in the main lodge?" he asked.

"Sure did," said I.

"Ever wonder how it died?"

"Just a guess, but somebody shot it?"

"Go take a look and show me the bullet hole."

So we walked the few yards from the guide's cabin, where we stayed, to the much larger lodge. The smaller place is much easier to heat, of course. I took the pelt down from the wall and checked it over, but couldn't find a bullet hole.

"Shot him in the eye?" I asked.

109

"Nope," John said, smiling.

"Texas heart shot?"

"Nope."

(A Texas heart shot, for the benefit of the uninitiated, is how a bullet might enter the body of an animal running directly away from you without it leaving a telltale bullet hole. Savvy?)

Well, I knew, since we were fifty air miles from a road, that the chances of this wolverine being roadkill were fairly remote.

"I give up," I told John.

"Crescent wrench," he said.

It seems that one lonely, cold winter's night, when the moon was out on the snow bright as near daylight, John was visiting the former owner of the lodge, Nick Botner. And, as sometimes happens in Alaska when someone comes to spend the night, and no one is driving anywhere later, there were liquid refreshments served after dinner. In fact, there were so many liquid refreshments served that a fairly good time was being had all the way around. They had rewritten the lyrics to some of Verdi's best arias to make them better fit a back-alley culture, and had designed new dances that Balanchine never dreamed of even after a pickle-eating contest. That's when John looked out the window onto the frozen lake in the magic of moonlight, and saw it.

"Wolverine!" John said. Sure enough, there was a wolverine out toward the center of the lake, hopping along in that characteristic hump-hump gait of theirs.

"Let's get him!" said Nick.

So the two of them stumbled out of the lodge to the snowmachine shed, jumped on the old Skidoo, and took off at the equivalent of drunken light speed after the midnight visitor. Before long, they were gaining pretty good on the wolverine.

"Shoot him!" Nick, who was in front, driving, yelled to John.

"Don't have a gun," yelled John.

"Look in the tool kit!" yelled Nick.

So John looked in the tool kit and the most lethal thing he found was a crescent wrench. Brandishing it high over his head, John, the terror of the North, was swept in closer and closer to the prey. Nick brought the snow machine alongside the wolverine, and the wolverine jumped at it.

You see, that's the problem with hunting wolverines. They hunt back. They are known to attack such things as moose, Cessna 210s, stationary cabins, highway bridges, and the Alaska Railroad. Two drunks on a snow machine was only a preliminary bout for this northern devil.

John was leaning out to swing the wrench when the wolverine jumped at them. So John straightened up, brought his arm down as hard as he could through thin air, and the wolverine stuck his head directly into the path of his swing.

BLAP!

That wolverine went end over end across the ice, and lay there dead.

When they checked again in the morning, armed to the teeth and sober this time, the wolverine had managed to stay dead all night, so they skinned it and as far as I know, the hide is still hanging on the wall of Stephan Lake Lodge.

I still think I'll use a rifle.

JEEP AND THE GRANDFATHERS
FICTION

→

W hen I'm thinking of wheres and whens and hows, my Norwegian ancestry takes over. When it came to dealing with facts and problems and logistics, it was hard to beat my grandfather, Roald Jepsen. He was one of the kindest men I ever knew and also the most practical.

Gramps, it was said, built the best sluice boxes in the gold fields. When you wanted a sluice box where the riffles always sat down in the slots without a wiggle, you went to Roald Jepsen and asked him for one. He just asked you how big you wanted it and that was it. Miners who had one of his sluice boxes showed them off to visitors like signed pieces of art.

Gramps built sluice boxes that captured gold, boats that didn't leak, and, in the days before everybody went nuts over aluminum, pack frames that never rubbed sores and hung just right.

His tools were always sharp. Their handles never broke or wore away. The doors on his cabin always fit exactly, despite weather changes. His roof never leaked.

When you had a problem in the bush, Gramps always took the practical approach.

"First," he used to say, "you sit down on a log. Then you think, and you think logically and you gotta think right. What is it you need? How many different ways are there of reasonably getting the job done with the tools and materials you have on hand?

"When, boy, you figure which one would be the best way to go, then you do it. Say you got a broken leg in the mountains? What would you do?"

And so I'd play the familiar game with him while he worked with a spokeshave or drawknife on a choice piece of wood. He'd work and listen, and I'd imagine myself in the woods with a broken leg. Then I'd start telling him some of the things I could do. He'd listen, nod and say "good" now and then, which always sounded a bit like "goot," and encourage me.

"You got a broken leg, how many things you gotta worry about?"

"Two," I'd say. "Take care of the leg and get help."

"Good start," he'd say. "But I think four things."

He stopped and counted on his fingers. "One, get that leg splinted. Take care of your health, right. Two, you need some sort of shelter to get after you fix your leg. Don't do any good to have a good leg and freeze to death, right? Three, you need to find food and fix a way to cook it. Four, when you're all set up so you don't need to go nowhere, then you figure a way to signal or get yourself out of the woods."

He'd look at me. "You gotta think, boy. If you think, you're always going to be ahead of the man who doesn't."

So I've tried to do that. Each time a problem comes up, I try to run it through the checklist that Gramps taught me. What are the various things that could happen? What do I want to do about it? What do I want to do about it first? How many ways are there to accomplish this? Which of these would work best?

This method has kept me out of trouble many times and has gotten me out of trouble a few times when I couldn't avoid getting into it. I miss that good-natured old man with his missing teeth and his gray hair and his laughter.

Sometimes late at night, though, when I'm this tired, my mind seems to belong to the Athabascan half of my ancestry. And when I hunt, it goes back to about a half-and-half balance. The white-guy half knows some good recipes for cooking a meal for a hunter in the field. The Indian-guy half finds game, sometimes, in a special way.

Chulyen, where are you now? Off to the places only ravens know about? Or are you picking through the debris of the alley behind Fourth Avenue, listening to country music and fights?

I remember you, Chulyen. It was the day when there was tracking snow and I was ten and Chada let me take the army rifle.

"You must not hurt the moose," my Chada, my Grandfather George, had said. "You must kill it or leave it alone."

I was carrying that heavy rifle and I looked up from beneath my marten-skin cap and nodded. We had gone maybe a quarter mile from his moose camp and a raven flew across our path, his wings beating that breathless sound as he crossed.

Chada nudged me. "Say good morning to him," he said.

"Why?"

"Because," he said, "it is to bring you good luck and keep Raven happy. Maybe he will show you a moose today."

"Good luck?"

Grandfather shrugged and grinned, the way I do these days. "It is kind of a nice old way of doing things, don't you think? And it doesn't hurt, does it?"

About that time, the raven turned from being on our right and flew back across our path to the left.

"Good morning, Raven," I said.

"Tell him you'll leave the gut pile for his children," Chada said.

"I'll leave the gut pile for your children," I called.

"And the eyes."

"That sounds awful."

"The eyes."

"And the eyes, too, Raven."

My grandfather smiled. "Maybe he'll like you."

As we walked along about half an hour later, we saw a raven flying down toward a creek from the alder thickets where we were.

"Chulyen," Grandfather said, nodding.

It may even have been the same one that had crossed our path earlier. It may have been another one. Alaska is full of ravens. But this one was flying that slow, deliberate way ravens have and heading down toward the creek.

Without saying anything more, Chada nudged me and pointed in the direction the bird went. He motioned for me to keep silent, too, and we started down toward the creek.

I heard the moose in the thicket along the creek and we worked our way silently, a step at a time, down from one spruce tree to another until we were about fifty yards from where the sound was coming. He motioned for me to stop and get ready and held his finger to the mouth again for silence. Quietly, I worked the bolt of the army rifle until a cartridge was loaded into the chamber, then flipped on the safety. I put my left hand around a skinny spruce tree and stuck my thumb out to the right. I laid the fore end of the rifle across that, got the rifle comfortably settled, and waited.

Then he stepped out. I had seen moose many times in my ten years, of course, but this was the biggest moose ever in the world because it was my moose.

I could hear in my mind Chada's admonition not to hurt him, so I put the sights on the exact spot where the spine crosses the shoulder blades, took off the safety, and squeezed the trigger.

The giant's four feet folded up against his body in midair and he hit the ground right there and it was his final place. It was my first moose, and he wasn't hurt, and it was the best day of my life.

After the moose died, Grandfather taught me to say a prayer of thanks to the moose for his meat. He pointed, and the raven was sitting in the top of a spruce tree about a hundred yards away.

His children got fat that day.

Since that day, I have had a special affection for Chulyen. When I hunt, his children eat. Sometimes when he crosses my path, it is a lucky day. Sometimes it isn't.

One morning I was tired, broke, out of work, and the truck broke down and I was hitchhiking to Anchorage. It was snowing like silt in a summer river and I'd been standing out on the highway for an hour with no car coming by. Just then a raven flew past.

"Chulyen!" I called out, laughing. "Good morning! Are you going to bring me luck today?"

He flew on his way, and I chuckled for about five minutes in the snowstorm.

That was when Bob Gordon picked me up and drove me to Anchorage. He gave me a twenty-dollar bill, fed me a steak dinner, and told me I could work as chore boy in his hunting camp for the rest of the season. That was how I got my start guiding.

I always say good morning to ravens. It is kind of a nice old way of doing things. And it doesn't hurt.

I could have used some of Raven's confidence that night, but I didn't find any. The underlying beat of Anchorage didn't help any, either. Not with a boy from the Bush who just wanted to smell the smoke from his own stovepipe and hear nothing but the soft popping of the dried birch chunks in the heater. I thought about my dogs. I thought about hunting camp. I thought about the sweetness of Ravel's music, I thought of Betsy then and smiled and dozed a bit until the light made it too embarrassing to stay in bed.

GHOST COON
OF TOMÉ

We've trailed him for a decade now
But never a shot's been fired,
As we chase raccoons through the desert night
Until the dogs get tired

Sometimes they tree, sometimes they lose
But the dogs enjoy the chase
We have our fun 'til the night is done
And the sunlight ends the race

Now the Ghost Coon lives on the wild east side
Of our magic Rio Grande
He waits for the hounds as they make their rounds
Up and down the bosque land

We treed him once and let him go
We treed him ten times more
He grew enthralled by the midnight bawl
Of the hounds on the river's shore
Just what there is in the cold night song
That thrills the old scamp so

We'll talk and dream and ask and scheme
But will never really know
It's been four years, four winters now
Since we've put him up a tree
But still we try as the hound dogs cry
And the Ghost Coon tries to flee

Oh, he craves the chase, far more than food
He's proven all along
He makes them run, and gives them fun
And loves the midnight song

He waits each night for the eager dogs
As he leaves his scented trace
We know he's there in the damp night air
Ready for the race

He takes us through the neighbor's yards
He awakens sleeping folks
Through chicken pens and soggy fens
He plays his nighttime jokes

If the dogs work hard and use their heads
And the Ghost Coon feels the heat
He'll often land in the Rio Grande
And swim to their defeat

When the dogs run four coon trails
All at once in the nightly fun
It's just the Ghost as he puts the most
Confusion in his run

We've cussed his name, but all the same
He's kinda fun to chase
His eyes glow red and we've often said
He's the devil in a masked face

But down the trail, if the Ghost should fail
It wouldn't be the same
And we'd hope, for one, that he'd raise a son
To play our midnight game
Dogs and men love a hopeless cause
A game that's fun to play
We need this test, to try our best
With the Ghost Coon of Tomé

TROUBLE
ON TRAIL

⸻⸻⸻⸻⟶

I n November of 1970, partly as a way to raise money for
a children's home in Anchorage, and partly to get me
out of the office once again, I attempted to bring the
first quart of oil down the pipeline route by dog team. Today
a haul road goes all the way up there and there are camps
and even the occasional gas pump along the way. But things
were pretty primitive then. Scattered camps, no pipeline
construction started yet, and the only means of transportation between the camps was helicopter and a big tractor-
like contraption that ran on inflated rubber bladders called
a Rollagon. At that pre-pipeline point, there were wells at
Prudhoe Bay on the North Slope with more being drilled,
but no roads and no pipeline. There were just mountains of
the forty-eight-inch pipe stacked there waiting for the official hokeydoke. Most of the men working in the more remote
camps, like Sagwon and Happy Valley, were there to do test
drilling to see where the tundra would best support the pipe,
and to make surveys of the area. The Brooks Range, at that
point, was still largely unexplored, and I can tell you from
personal experience that in winter it was (and still is) a nasty
vertical frozen rock pile.

I will pause at this point to tell you one of the funniest stories I ever heard about helicoptering on the Slope. Why? Well, it doesn't have a thing to do with what follows, but it's really funny and I feel like telling it.

One very cold winter morning, a pilot new to the Slope landed outside the buildings at Happy Valley Camp, turned off his helicopter, and went inside for breakfast. He got his meal, then went out with the survey crew that he was to fly to a mountain top that morning. They climbed into the back and buckled up, and so did he.

The missing pilot was cussed thoroughly by the men huddled there, freezing their farkles off in the back of the copter. What happened to him? Where was he? Finally, the pilot, who had been posing as a passenger, unbuckled his seat belt, saying, "Hell, anyone can fly one of these damn things. I'll do it myself!" and he climbed up front and hit the ignition switch.

It took twenty minutes to get the survey crew back inside the helicopter.

Dogsled: A True Tale of the North, my first book, was published in 1977. It chronicled two dog-mushing trips I took for *The Anchorage Daily News* so I could get out of the office. The first trip was such a paper-seller that they "demoted" me from city editor to reporter (with a raise) and gave me the title Resident Adventurer. Well, you just couldn't have a better job in Alaska. It was great.

This second big dogsled trip didn't work out as well as the first one, but here I am in my sixties now, so at least that part of it turned out all right, as I was twenty-eight at the time. Here is a segment of Dogsled.

The deep diesel bawl of a wolf, joined by another in a higher pitch, woke me before dawn. I lighted the Coleman burner and fixed tea and ham for breakfast.

It was Friday, November 20, and the world outside the igloo was white and dark at the same time—and very cold.

Listening to the radio transmissions between the camps with my walkie-talkie, I learned it was twenty-five below at Sagwon, my destination for the day.

At twenty below and colder, there seems to be a definite feel in the air that isn't noticed at warmer temperatures. It is a total chill, as though a man left a sauna and stepped into a cold storage plant. At this temperature, exposed flesh freezes in sixty seconds, so the trick is not to expose any flesh. My full-knit hood was again put into play, with the addition of a "Slope mask" given me by the foreman at Crazy Horse Camp. It is a felt-lined leather mask, with slots for the mouth and eyes.

It took a while to reconvert the roof of the igloo into tarp and snowshoes, and load and lash the gear on the sled. It was beginning to turn pink in the south as I walked along the picket chain, retrieving the dogs. By morning, all that's visible on the picket line are eleven little geysers of warm breath emerging through finger-sized holes. The musher must reach down through the snow at each geyser, grab the submerged dog, and pull him, unwilling and shivering, into the cold air.

With the team harnessed, I walked ahead of Tanya with snowshoes, packing a trail through the soft snow. Unlike experienced freight teams, however, they didn't know enough to follow me, and I was forced to walk back to the team and drive them forward to the end of the packed trail. Then it was back to the front again, and pack more trail.

After half a mile of this, we reached a slight rise in the snow, where the wind had blown a good crust. Off came the snowshoes, and the team struck off at a good trot across the glazed surface while a tired musher rode the runners. The break came just in time to save my flagging spirits, because breaking trail is tough work, and I wasn't used to the awkward shuffling gait necessary with the big twelve-by-sixty snowshoes.

The dogs picked up some speed across the glaze, pulling away from the south buttress of the Franklin Bluffs. Shortly, through the expanse of white, some gently rolling hills began to show up ahead. These I knew to be the Sag Hills, the northernmost foothills of the Brooks Range. Reaching them was a particularly tasty goal for me. When we reached the base of those hills, we would have accomplished the first solo dog sled crossing of the North Slope at that longitude. I urged the dogs on further and faster.

Gazing down the long towline ahead of me, I checked on each dog's progress on the team. For once, all eleven dogs were running without a tangle across the glaze, and seemed to enjoy it.

Then I noticed something strange about George . . .

George, a pretty Siberian named for champion musher George Attla, had begun to weave drunkenly in his traces. Then he hung back in his harness for a second and flopped on his side.

I slammed on the brake, and jammed the hook into the snow. Running to the young dog, I unsnapped him from the neckline so he wouldn't choke, and picked him up. There was no breath in him, his eyes had begun to glaze, and the usually pink flesh of the mouth showed traces of cyanotic blue. I rolled him over in my arms and began to blow into his mouth. It was hard to make a seal around his mouth with the heavy mittens on, so I pulled them off and tried again. This helped quite a bit. With my bare hands, I was able to make a much better seal around the long pointed muzzle.

Trying not to hurry, as feelings of panic and regret engulfed me, I continued for long steady minutes with the resuscitation.

Feeling a cold nose in my face, I looked up to see Doc, George's partner, whining and looking anxiously at what I was doing.

Doc was a big square-jawed cross between a husky and a St. Bernard (as nearly as I could guess) and he and George had become close partners. Doc was named for Dr. Roland Lombard, who in real life is the friend and perennial mushing rival of George Attla.

My left hand, totally exposed to the cold for long minutes, now began to stiffen. Unwillingly, I laid the dead body of the little Siberian on the snow and forced my frozen hand back into the mitten.

But the hand didn't hurt, and wasn't on my mind. I was hurt and angry at the injustice of this dog's death. At least when Scarface died, there was a reason. George, a young dog, had pulled and felt good, and had shown no signs of sickness until just a very few seconds before his death.

Just as I laid him down, there was a hum in the sky, and the big Wien jet streaked with its low drone toward Prudhoe Bay. Aboard that warm airplane, pretty girls would be serving coffee to lounging people. At my feet lay the lifeless form of a little sled dog. My tears froze to my face.

Removing his harness and collar, I kicked a hole in the snow, tumbled the remains in, and covered it as best I could. The ravens would find it anyway, but I'd at least make them work for it.

An hour's mushing later, the glazed surface disappeared, and the lead dogs floundered in powder snow three feet deep. By now, we had swung in an arc, carrying us close to the Sag River again. The hills were upon us, and we would take the river or its edge along the side of the hills until we reached the crossing to Sagwon. From the soft miasmas of fog rising from the river, it was obvious that overflow still existed, ruling out a return to the ice.

Strapping on the snowshoes, I set out ahead of the team, stomping the soft powder as hard as I could. My heavy clothes, and the constant trodding work, soon had me gasping for breath. The steam from my body rose out through the openings in the winter gear, and hung in a frozen vapor around my body as I went.

Pack, pack, pack . . .

The work went on. I would break trail for several hundred yards, then return to the team and drive them the short distance to powder snow again. Then the snowshoer went back to his task.

Pack, pack, pack . . .

The vibrato of a helicopter interrupted my work, and I looked up to see the familiar Bell Jetranger of the pipeline camps. I welcomed my opportunity to rest for a few minutes. Pulling out my walkie-talkie, I talked to the pilot, who asked if I was all right. He put my position as being about nine miles north of Sagwon Camp.

"You're right on course," he said. "We thought we'd land for a minute."

"Come ahead," I said.

What I wanted right then was a cold drink of water, but the thermos of hot coffee they brought more than made up for the lack of water. Two men aboard the chopper took pictures of the team while I told the pilot of George's death.

"I'll fly over tomorrow again," the pilot promised, "but you'll probably make Sagwon tonight."

"I sure hope so," I said, "but there's a lot of trail to break first."

"Well, good luck," they said.

The jet engine began its whine, grew louder, and the snow blew up in huge clouds around the machine. The dogs turned their backs to the propwash as they would on a storm, and the chopper lifted lazily into the air and hummed south toward Happy Valley Camp, eighteen miles south of Sagwon.

When this sole reminder of the modern world had vanished, it left a very lonely feeling behind. All about was just a quiet white world. The total silence and distance had an almost narcotic effect. More and more, the team and I seemed to be miserable ants, crawling across a belligerent white cold surface.

Back I went to the snowshoes. Pack, pack, pack . . .

When I returned to the team this time, they all began sniffing the air with nervous agitation. Driving the dogs, I noticed a reluctance of many of them to move at all. This seemed quite strange, as we hadn't gone far enough that day for them to be tired. Tanya especially was hesitant about going. She finally

125

yielded to my command, and walked quietly and slowly, look-ing from side to side. Sometimes she'd stop and stick her nose in the air. Most of the team followed after her.

Finally she quit. She just looked back at me once, then began digging a hole in the snow. Several others began follow-ing her actions.

Walking ahead, I grabbed Tanya and tried to drag her for-ward. Not only would she not take a step, but none of the nine dogs behind her would, either. It is possible to drag one eighty-five-pound dog, but not ten of them. The minute I released her, she went back to digging her hole in the snow. All the others were doing the same by this time, so there was no sense in trying to go any farther.

I spread out the picket chains, then unharnessed and dragged each dog to the chain. As soon as they had been fas-tened, they dug frantically under the snow. Had I been a bit smarter, I would have paid more attention, but I begrudgingly went about my tent staking and unloading of the sled, think-ing of warm Sagwon Camp, now a scant eight miles away, and the bed and food that waited there.

The temperature dropped remarkably fast, and I noticed the exposed noses of the dogs were covered with thick frost as I fed them. My breath drifted to the sled, and froze to it. It was becoming painful to breathe.

Then I noticed the total absence of sound. It was the deliberate silence of the North—the stunned, half-quivering silence of the theatre audience as the house lights dim.

Moving in silent haste, I shoved my sleeping bag and valu-ables into the tent, and turned to begin my igloo, but I did it with a crawling fear. Something was going to happen. The stage was set, the audience was afraid of the outcome. I felt the fear rising inside, and cursed myself for the weakness.

Then the storm hit.

The whiteout dropped first, obscuring the dogs, and concentrating the range of vision to the tent and the sled. It was silent and deliberate as it went about its work, concealing its coming deeds from the eyes of the world.

I stood there for the few seconds it took to drop, watching it swallow my dogs and the front part of the sled.

The first blast of wind tumbled me into a snowdrift and snapped one of the tent poles like a twig. Gasping for breath, I quickly shed the snowshoes, and used one of them to replace the broken tent pole. Then I crawled into the tiny tunnel-flap on the lee side of the tent. Pulling off my mukluks, I crawled into the six-pound down sleeping bag, which was guaranteed to minus seventy degrees.

When the initial shock of the blast had worn off, I searched through my duffle bag and found the Coleman burner, then pulled out some dehydrated food for dinner. I could only keep my hands unmittened for a few seconds each time, as the cold would go quickly through the light "monkey face" gloves and freeze them.

When I tried to pump and light the burner, nothing happened. I shook it, but just heard a sludgy sloshing inside. When the reservoir was opened, I poured out a few lumps of white gas in a form resembling catsup. Later, other Alaskans told me that Blazo does this at minus forty, but I had to learn the hard way.

Fishing again in the duffle bag, I located several cans of Sterno that I had brought along on a whim. It was fortunate that I did, for the Sterno began to burn immediately, and did well for the several hours that it lasted.

It was most difficult heating anything over the Sterno, due to the difference in temperature between the bottom of the pan and the top. Nevertheless, I was able to melt snow and get the water at least warm, then soak the dried food in it, making it chewy. Several hours later, dinner of soggy crunchy beef and noodles, and three bars of chocolate was completed. I washed it down with lukewarm water just as the last of the Sterno burned away.

The wind picked up. It blew on the tent until I felt sure we would all be blown to Greenland, but enough snow had drifted around the tent by this time that it was held down firmly.

In fact, holding down the tent created one of my biggest problems. With the tent walls crushing down, space inside was becoming nonexistent. I couldn't afford to get buried by the storm, as certain suffocation would follow.

How long would the storm last?

The one I had been caught in at Deadhorse lasted fifteen hours, but the men kept saying we were overdue for a good blow. A "blow" in this country sometimes lasts five and six days, with the average storm lasting about three days.

As if that weren't enough, I began to notice a light layer of powdery snow covering the duffle and my other gear inside the tent. Looking down toward my feet, I discovered the source. A tiny hole on the windward side of the tent, smaller than a sharp pencil puncture, was allowing a fine spray of snow inside. It resembled the spray from an aerosol can. It was located too far up the tent wall for me to plug it with some gear, so I draped a piece of tarp over most of my gear.

By keeping the flashlight, walkie-talkie, and rescue gear inside my sleeping bag, I could keep the batteries warm enough to work.

Every hour or so, I would turn on the walkie-talkie, carefully poking the antenna out the breathing hole of my sleeping bag. Until late that night, I heard nothing.

At about one a.m., I picked up a radio signal. Happy Valley Camp was calling Crazy Horse.

They spoke for several minutes about what machinery the one camp needed from the other, and then they mentioned the weather.

"How is it at your place?" one said.

"Blowin' bad," said the other, "about forty-five below with sixty-knot winds gusting to around eighty."

"Yeah," said the first, "dropped to minus fifty for about an hour, but is back to forty-five now."

Then they signed off, and left the tent in silence. Having a pretty good memory of the chill factor chart, I knew that the rating didn't go that low. Wind drops the temperature of an area at a certain rate. Wind robs the body of heat much more quickly in cold weather. Therefore, when it is zero degrees with a ten-mile-per-hour wind, the weather chills a person as much as though it were calm outside and twenty below. A person will freeze as quickly in that circumstance as he would at the lower temperature.

The chart goes down to minus 148 degrees, and the storm outside went beyond. It doesn't matter, though, because at chill factors of 148 below, which is180 degrees of frost, flesh will freeze almost immediately, and the lungs get seared by the forced cold, causing death.

At first, the storm seemed rather exciting. Unlike the Sergeant Preston programs, though, the wind doesn't whistle in treeless areas, but keeps a constant "whoosh!" going outside the tent.

By now, the seriousness of my situation had begun setting in. Already, moisture was forming inside the sleeping bag. It would freeze when I would partially emerge to shove the gathering snow from the front flap. The ice would then melt when I sealed it up again, soaking my clothes. When I emerged the next time, I would find ice next to my skin. Time after time this went on until I was virtually encased in a thin sheet of ice. The only cure for this was to get the clothes dried out by a fire, but my hopes of that disappeared with the last few strawberry drops of Sterno.

The chilling of my body went on. The first two fingers of my left hand hadn't completely thawed since the dog died, and were stiff and useless like sticks of wood. My bad ear from the first trip was alternately freezing and thawing, creating an intense burning pain when it thawed. In a way, that was good, because the pain helped me stay awake—and I dared not fall asleep.

The old wives' tale about falling asleep and freezing to death worked well in Jack London's excellent story "To Build a Fire," but the truth is, if a man is in that cold a situation, without heat from an outside source, he'll freeze to death whether he's awake or asleep. In my circumstances, however, I was in danger of being smothered by blowing snow, and only my hourly diligent few minutes of scooping and pounding kept me uncovered. The task became increasingly difficult as the night wore on. Several inches of the finely-sifted powder lay on every piece of gear I had, and I could no longer open the front flap to shove it out. My fingers had lost their capacity for fine manipulation.

When the first waves of dizziness came over me, close to morning, I knew I was in deep trouble. When hypothermia causes the body temperature to drop, the mind plays tricks on a man.

I told myself, "Whatever happens, you will not leave this tent! Nothing can live outside this tent! Stay inside!"

As a person about to go on a bender would tell himself, "No matter how drunk you get, you will not drive home!" the message stayed with me.

Of the hours of delirium that followed, I remember very few things. At the outset, I was determined to keep my mind working. I found my journal in a parka pocket and wrote several shaky sentences before the hand ceased to function. With my left hand, I pulled the pen out of the right, and then beat the hand flat until it slipped back into the big mitten. Writing was obviously out of the question.

What I needed to do was read, but I couldn't turn the pages of the little book I had brought. Fishing around under the dusty snowpile again, I came upon a can of Spam in the foodstuffs. Eating was not in the cards, as it had frozen to a brick, but the can had writing on it, and I intended to read it.

Whenever I felt the silliness of what the Indians call the "cold drunk," or *deska'ss coday*, come over me, I would read the can of Spam. This seemed to help some, but more and more quickly, the words would fade, and I found myself thinking, "What do I care if Spam is the registered trademark of a pork product processed by the Geo. A. Hormel Company in Austin, Minnesota?"

To keep my mind off the cold of my body, I thought of other things. I recall wondering what the Spam plant in Austin, Minnesota looked like. Then I would remember that Minnesota gets cold in the winter, and I would get cold again.

The cold that comes in an Arctic storm is not, as scientists would have you believe, merely the absence of heat. The cold of the North is a terrible sledge that slams the senses, renders strong men useless, and weak men dead. It drives the nearly indestructible moose into hiding. The cold is everywhere, like smoke, and seeps in openings in clothing and bedding you weren't aware you had. Everywhere it finds flesh, it numbs like Novocain. It is a total condition. It strikes everything, and only the brave flames of a fire can protect a man.

But I had no fire.

The jelling of the Coleman fuel for the stove was a real sore point with me. For the best part of an hour, during lucid moments, I mapped out the nasty letter I was going to send to the company. When polished, it was short and to the point:

A tent
Eight miles from Sagwon
Alaska

Dear Mr. Coleman:

This is to inform you that the fuel you sell for your little Coleman one-burner camp stove doesn't work at less than forty degrees below zero Fahrenheit.

I hope you realize that I may very well freeze to death because of the failure of your fuel to burn. In the future,

*please refrain from showing nothing but happy campers in
the pamphlets you distribute. Show a picture of someone in a
stupid Army tent in the foothills of the stupid Brooks Range
freezing to stupid death because he couldn't do anything with
the stupid fuel but spread it on a piece of stupid bread.*

*In short, Mr. Coleman, and before I enter my
terminal stages of hypothermia, I would just like to say
(and please excuse the pun) that I wish your fuel was
made of Sterno stuff!*

With warm regards but a cold stove,
Slim Randles

With the letter totally put together in my mind, I began to
wonder what effect the letter would have on the future of cold-
weather camping. Would Mr. Coleman immediately call in his
top engineers and say, "Well boys, here's Slim's letter, now let's
get on with it, and come up with a stove fuel that can be used
all year round in beautiful Eight-Miles-From-Sagwon."

Actually, I believed my chances were better of receiving the following reply.

Dear Mr. Randles:

*In regard to your letter of Nov. 22, 1970, thanks for your
interest in Coleman camping products.*

*Also, why don't you do your camping in the summer
like sane people do?*

Sincerely,
Mr. Coleman

The thought of receiving that letter from Mr. Coleman discouraged me from ever writing the first one, so I guess we'll
never know.

But my preoccupation with the correspondence between
the Coleman people and myself was short-lived. Before much
longer, my eyes wouldn't focus properly—the tiny muscles

needed for the operation had ceased to function. The panic of a person suddenly blinded came on me. I even began to miss reading the can of Spam. In fact, that can of Spam became very important to me. I shielded it against the cold inside my sleeping bag with my other valuables, as though it were a talisman of proper sight.

In my half-lucid frame of mind, I felt the aircraft beacon and considered turning it on. After all, I thought, this was an emergency, and I could remember that I was only to use it in case of emergency. Then, trying hard, I was able to reason that the pipeline men knew I was in trouble, and they also knew my approximate location, and they couldn't fly in this storm anyway.

I was totally cut off. They couldn't come at all.

After that, I remember little except vague dreams that would come across my mind as I drifted in and out of consciousness.

Always, though, I remembered to stay inside the tent. "Nothing can live outside the tent!"

With the illogical logic known to us in dreams, I then reasoned that the dogs had all died. They were outside the tent. Nothing outside the tent could live. Therefore the dogs were now dead. I turned on the walkie-talkie once and heard nothing. The men at the camps were dead. The camps were outside the tent. If they were dead, then everything outside the tent was dead.

What would I do? This problem kept flashing through what was left of my thinking processes. I began to drag in wisps of thought and swirl them together into a misty plan. If the storm let up before I died, I would walk south until I found a warm climate, and build a house and find something to eat if I could. But I would have to get warm . . . that was first . . . I would have to get warm.

All my friends and family had died in the storm . . . I knew that by now. They weren't in the tent. If only the tent were bigger, I could have some people in it with me, and we could all live. . . .

I barely heard the chopper's engine approaching, some thirty-two hours after I had last seen it. The men's hands were gentle and firm as they dug down and pulled me out of the tent. I recall asking them, when we were in the heated helicopter and they gave me sips of coffee, how they managed to stay alive in the storm. Did they have tents? They were kind, and said I'd be in a warm camp pretty soon.

Later, I was to learn that Big Mike had somehow wrapped the picket line around a front leg, cutting off circulation. The leg was amputated in Fairbanks.

The pilot had flown even before it was totally safe to do so. The temperature was minus eighteen, with a twenty-five-knot wind blowing when they found me, putting the chill factor at seventy-five degrees below zero.

The men had found me by spotting two inches of tent that still showed above the snow, and the red-painted driving bow of the big freight sled. Some men later flew out and took the whole team and the equipment to Sagwon, and several days later, to Fairbanks.

Even before "Doc" Jose Harrison called a halt to the trip, I knew it was over. George dead. Mike's leg gone. Two of my fingers in pretty bad shape.

It was over.

WHEN YOU JUST
CAN'T LOSE. . . .

———————————————————▶

They say hindsight is always 20/20, don't they? Well, if that's true, we should've forgotten all about taking Lew Erickson hunting in Alaska, bundled him onto the nearest jet, and flown him straight to Las Vegas.

When you can't lose, you can't lose.

It wasn't Lew's fault that he was the luckiest hunter who ever lived. You can't blame a guy for that, even if it makes the other hunters in camp feel a little hurt and left out. Oh, they did just fine out there at George Palmer's camp on the Dillinger River. Everyone had a good time and took game and we laughed for ten days and felt great. But Lew was to be my hunter during that time, and I just had no idea what that hunt would be like. Not every guide gets a Lew, even in a lifetime of guiding.

And he was certainly a nice guy. If I recall correctly Lew owned some kind of business in Santa Cruz, California, and was really looking forward to this Alaska hunt. And why? Because he'd always dreamed of taking a big moose.

Well, that's wonderful, of course, but there are other game animals in Alaska that are interesting too, but Lew really wanted that moose. Moose . . . well, let's just say that moose aren't usually the most *challenging* game animal in

135

Alaska. Not that we're always tripping over them, mind you, but they are plentiful and we felt confident that Lew would be taking one home.

It's Morning One on a ten-day hunt. After a good breakfast in the dark there in main camp on the Dillinger, Lew and I start out to see if we can find his moose. The way I was figuring it, then, I'd get him that moose first, then we could both relax and see what other game we could rustle up for the remainder of the hunt.

So we walk out to the bank of the silty and icy Dillinger, and I look upstream to the peaks at the headwaters because the first rays of the sun are just striking the snow banks up there and it sure is pretty.

And those two full-curl Dall rams up there sure were pretty, too.

I hopped around and got out the spotting scope and set it up. I was excited, and Lew could tell. But I don't think he really understood why.

They were beauties. At least thirty-six-inchers, both of them.

"Lew, do you have a sheep tag?"

"Sure, Slim. I've got tags for everything."

"There's your ram," I said. "Let's see if we can put a sneak on him."

"Well . . . okay, if you say so," he said. "No moose up there, I guess."

"No, but look at those rams! Let's see if we can get on them."

So for the next hour and a half we climbed straight up over rock outcroppings, until I figured we should be at about the same elevation as those sheep. Then we put a quiet, patented power sneak on the last place we'd seen them. What are the chances they'd still be there? Remote. But those were beautiful rams.

And they still were. We stuck our heads up and there they were, twenty-five yards away, looking at us.

"Take the one on the left," I whispered. And he did. We got some close-up photos of the ram's partner, who hung around for a few minutes, too, and then I was busy for quite a while in the unzipping and subdividing business. Lew was disappointed that this sheep detour took up the entire day, by the time we got all that meat and horns and cape packed down to camp. But he was gentleman enough not to complain about it. As I told him, on a guided hunt in great sheep country, a hunter has a 25 percent chance of taking a legal ram, and he had taken a great ram on the first day of his hunt.

And that moose? Well, there's tomorrow, Lew. There's tomorrow.

So, in order to free up the morrow for moose pursuits, I fleshed that sheep cape on into the evening as Lew watched, along with Joe Palmer, George's dad. Old Joe was a real character. A miner from the mountains of California. He smoked his pipe and philosophized greatly and made camp a colorful and wonderful place to be.

This was never as obvious as it was on Morning Two.

We had a little problem on Morning Two. Fog. I emerged from the bull tent and found my way to the cook tent by Braille. The ceiling was right down on the floor, and it was a minor miracle that all the guides and hunters found the coffee pot that morning.

The other guides and hunters in camp were satisfied that this would be what we called a Louis L'Amour Day, which means stay in your bunk and read a good Western. Alaska's crummy weather is the reason the hunts are a minimum of ten days.

A little aside here. Years later I interviewed Louis L'Amour at his home in Beverly Hills and I mentioned calling them Louis L'Amour Days and it tickled him.

But Lew wasn't a guy to sit and read when all of outdoor Alaska was just sitting outside that tent. I don't care if you can't see your feet, we're *hunting!*

137

I tried explaining to Lew that for moose hunting, the drill is to climb to an observation point, glass miles of country until you see a moose, then go get him. This is hard to do when you can't see each other out there.

"But what will we hunt, then?" he asked.

I sighed. Okay, I knew Lew was one of these guys who eats alfalfa sprouts and runs the marathon before breakfast back at home each day, so I figured we're in for a hike. Sometimes you have to kinda take the edge off a hunter before he is content to sit and glass the countryside.

Before I could answer his question, Old Joe Palmer piped up. "Do you have a wolf tag, Lew?"

Lew looked in his portfolio and said he did. He said he had tags for everything.

"Well, I wish you'd go get that danged wolf that's been stealing my whisky bottle," he said. We all laughed, because we knew Joe's daughter-in-law was most likely responsible for any whisky-bottle relocation around there.

"I had that bottle stashed in a squirrel hole out there past the bull tent," Joe said, "and that danged ol' wolf came along and stole it. Why don't you go get him today?"

Well, there had been wolf tracks out on the sand bars in the river lately, actually.

"Can we go get that wolf, Slim?" he asked.

"Uh . . . sure, Lew. If you've got a wolf tag, we can go try for him."

You don't see wolves in Alaska. Not unless you're flying and it's winter. Oh, you hear them sometimes, but see them? Nope. They don't like people.

So after breakfast, when the other guys were getting out the cards and the paperback books, Lew and Slim were getting ready for a little hike.

Off we went, down the riverbank. We'd stumbled our best through the fog for almost two hundred yards, I'd guess, when all of a sudden the fog pulled back and revealed . . . yep . . . a coal black wolf standing broadside twenty-five yards away.

While Lew was jacking a shell into the chamber, that wolf went into overdrive and Lew dumped it ass-over-teakettle just as it jumped a big log, about a hundred yards away. Prettiest running shot I've ever seen.

The other guys heard the shot from camp.

"Oh no," they said, quietly. "Slim shot him."

But no, that wasn't how things were, at all. There on the ground was a stone-dead female wolf, a gorgeous coal-black wolf, an actual, *real* Alaska timber wolf, measuring seven feet two inches, from her nose to the tip of her tail.

I skinned her out, draped the hide over my shoulders, and we were back in camp in time for the next pot of coffee. By the way, those wolves stink to high heaven. I had to throw my shirt away.

Then the fog lifted, and there I was in the trophy tent, fleshing a wolf pelt.

Lew stood there quietly, watching me work, and understanding that fleshing and salting were necessary, but looking outside at the wonderful visibility and wishing we were in full pursuit of Old Paddlehead.

What the odds are on a fair-chase hunter taking a wolf in daylight I don't know. Infinitesimal. I'm sure it's been done, but I've never even *heard* of another hunter doing it. I've always suspected that the State of Alaska sells wolf and wolverine tags to nonresident hunters simply to beef up the state coffers.

But Lew filled his tag that day, fair chase. We couldn't stop grinning.

On Morning Three, which dawned with great visibility, I thought I'd better quit fooling around with these rare trophy animals and go find Lew a moose. So we started off down the Dillinger River to a nice little lookout spot where I knew moose enjoyed hanging around.

We were ensconced on this little knoll there, glassing around, and right behind us was a blueberry flat, which is kinda like a meadow without grass. I kept turning around and looking at it. Something about it held my attention, and I turned around to face it, and motioned to Lew to do the same.

Now this next is something other hunters might scoff at, unless they've been in the bush for a long period of time. You have to be out there for quite a while, but when you have, you can almost *feel* the game. It's happened to me several times, and this morning was one of those times.

We're sitting there in prime moose stuff and yet there was this feeling. No sound, no sight, no smell of anything at all, please understand. Just a *feeling*. It's as though a guy is looking at a painting and saying, you know, what's missing right there in this corner of the painting is a . . . fill in the blank.

I whispered to Lew, "Do you have a grizzly tag?"

"Sure," he said. "I have a tag for . . ."

"Right, right. Well, put a shell in the chamber and put on the safety."

He looked at me strangely, but did as I asked, and I kept looking at a little hill on the opposite side of the blueberry flat, about 100 yards from us.

He looked at me strangely again, but by this time I was pointing at the hill, and right on cue out stepped a 750-pound grizzly. We waited until she reached the middle of the flat to be sure she didn't have cubs, and then Lew made another pretty shot.

So now it's Morning Four, after breakfast, and good ol' Guide Slim is out in the trophy tent fleshing and salting a grizzly hide the size of a coverlet for a queen-sized bed. It will take all day to do this right, which pretty much shoots any moose-hunting plans in the head, but hey, that's the way it goes. Lew is standing there, being polite and as patient as he can be for a guy who can't go moose hunting until tomorrow, and Old Joe Palmer is standing there, smoking his pipe and silently recalling some of the great miracles of all time, including water into wine, loaves and fishes, trails through the Red Sea, and hunting with Lew Erickson.

"So you think you'll be done by tomorrow, Slim?" Lew asked.

"Sure, Lew. We'll go after that moose in the morning."

He nodded his head. For the record here, at this point, let me explain that Lew eventually got that moose of his, on Morning Nine.

But back in that trophy tent, he wasn't looking all that optimistic. He'd been hunting four days so far and had taken three of the rarest animals in Alaska, but he hadn't even *seen* a moose yet.

It must have been very frustrating for Lew. But Old Joe summed it up nicely for the rest of us as he stood there watching me work that morning. "Say, Lew," Joe said, "do you have a rhino tag in there?"

"Well . . . no."

Old Joe nodded sagely. "Damn good thing."

BUNKHOUSE
BALLADS

---→

A bunkhouse is a strange American phenomenon, and one most of us don't think about very much. We all know what it is, of course. It's that cabin at a ranch or pack station or hunting camp where the single guys stay. The workers.

It's also the last remaining vestige of the Round Table of King Arthur, for it's here that the elite of the western world reside. For some it's for a few weeks during the gather, or a few months during hunting season. For others, it's home. It's the place where everything a cowboy has is stashed under his particular bunk. If there is anything in common in the bunkhouse, it's the chore of bringing in firewood, and communal access to the coffee pot.

The rules of bunkhouse living are simple:

a. If you read after the old guys want the light out, you must do it by flashlight inside your bedroll
b. If you snore, it is the responsibility of the others to plug their ears
c. No chamber pots in the bunkhouse. You get up and go outside, regardless of weather

d. Pets are allowed, as long as the pets aren't cats. Cats will fight with the dogs, who *are* allowed. Dogs who start fights are banished. The proper place for any pet is either on or under the owner's bunk, or lying quietly on the rug in the communal center of the room.

e. No one is to sit on anyone else's bunk, period, unless they are visiting and are invited to.

f. No one is to get into anyone else's gear for even a cigarette without first obtaining permission.

g. When a paperback novel is completely read, the reader will contribute it to the communal bookshelf. Even the dirty ones. In fact, *especially* the dirty ones.

h. If you buy cookies or doughnuts, you must buy enough for everyone.

i. If you don't like breathing tobacco smoke, it's your responsibility to move out. You must not open a window in cold weather.

j. While many women may be ravished during conversations in the bunkhouse, they must not be ravished there in real life. Go to town. Get a room. You can lie about it when you get back.

k. The oldest guy in the bunkhouse has seniority and gets to pick which calendar and pictures hang on the walls, regardless of taste. If the oldest guy dies or finds a better job, the oldest cowboy remaining shall have redecorating rights.

The American bunkhouse is a treasure trove of history, philosophy, education, chivalry, horsemanship, loyalty, politics, poverty, and falsehoods. Some bunkhouse residents are good at all of these simultaneously.

One memorable night at the pack station in Onion Valley, some of us younger guys were talking about some of the old outlaws of the West. Butch Cassidy was mentioned.

At that point, ol' Grant Dalton opened his eyes and nodded his head. "I liked ol' Butch," Grant said. "Saved me from a whippin' once when I was a kid."

Turned out it was true.

On another occasion, in a bunkhouse in the Alaska Range (but up there, since it's a tent, it's known as a "bull tent") the evening discussion centered around a pal who had died and of the fight several family members were having over who got his cabin.

One hunting guide then told us how the court would handle things and how the law specified taking care of property when a resident of Alaska died intestate.

Some of us thought intestate was one of those big freeways in the Lower 48 or was maybe scrotum-related, so we rolled over in bed and looked at this guide. He shrugged and said, "I was a lawyer once, a long time ago."

Rocky Earick, my old pack station pard, used to come up with the dad-gummedest philosophies while riding a horse through the mountains. He was quiet sometimes, and that's how we could tell he was ready to spring one on us. It takes a period of silence for a guy to gather up all his philosophical ideas and coagulate them into a usable nugget of true wisdom.

Just take for example one evening in the ranch bunkhouse near Independence during spring shoeing. The conversation had strayed over to where it usually went, meaning a careful and deliberate comparison of both the qualitative and quantitative anatomies of the waitresses at the Pines Café. Rocky didn't contribute to this, strangely enough, even though he was something of an authority in the field.

These conversations were usually sprinkled with vast admiration for certain women, such as "You know, I'd just like to take a little nip on the left-hand side, get lockjaw, and die of rug burn."

But when the comparisons of bra sizes had died down, and before anyone could get around to proper butt proportions, Rocky spoke.

"It's all them doctors' faults, you know," he said.

He looked around, but saw only puzzled looks. Evidently we weren't following the same train of thought that he was, since our trains seemed to be headed toward cute waitresses. So he explained.

"Remember how you used to be able to camp a party in Sixty Lakes Basin for a week and never see no backpackers anywhere? Hell yes, and just a few years ago, too.

"But now you ride up there and . . . *hell's bells* . . . it looks like L.A.! One guy had a generator in there and had electric lights in his tent."

"That's a fact," said Homer. "I seen it myself."

"Damn doctors!" said Rocky.

"Doctors?" one of us timidly asked.

"Why hell yes, doctors. Them doctors just keep on keeping people alive instead of letting them die, don't they? That's where all them people are coming from. Without doctors, we'd get Sixty Lakes Basin back. Maybe even Charlotte Lake!"

It's hard to argue with that.

There's one other rule in the bunkhouse that really isn't spoken about, but it's nevertheless recognized. That is, the old timers know they have to tolerate a certain amount of foolishness from the young guys, because they were young guys themselves once, and no one could ever be as foolish as they were back in those days.

The old guys also realize that for some of the youngsters, this is their first "home" away from Mama. This means they kinda flex their wings a bit on what is allowed and what isn't. The old guys make sure the wing flexing stays within reasonable bunkhouse bounds, of course, but there is a mountain-legal tolerance for fads built into bunkhouse life.

Like guitar playing.

One year at the pack station, all the young guys got guitars and the one guy in the bunkhouse who had asked someone about it was then designated to teach the rest of us the three chords. With three chords, you see, you can play rhythm for any Johnny Cash song written before 1980, and this was long before 1980. If you knew more than three chords, you were probably just putting on airs or were fond of folk music.

It was the old guys' responsibility to either remove their hearing aids or plug their ears, because the annual bunkhouse fad must be celebrated.

In some cases, however, there just weren't enough earplugs to go around.

As in Larry's case. Larry was the lover of the bunkhouse. He was a tall, good-looking guy who was even more popular with the Owens Valley girls than my pard Rocky was. And Rocky was no slouch.

Larry was the one who knew the three chords. I had joined the bunch, naturally, by shoeing a guy's horse in town and receiving in exchange one Sears Roebuck Silvertone f-hole guitar with a crack in the top and no strings. Had to send a guy to Bishop to get strings for it.

And while Larry knew just where to put his fingers on the fret board to make those three chords, his singing was more limited. In fact, he knew only one stanza of one song, and it only required two of the three chords. Thankfully, he remembered how to finger the unused chord so we could imitate Johnny Cash.

But Larry would sing his stanza any time anyone wanted him to, and many times when no one wanted him to. Here was his stanza:

"You don't know what lonesome is, 'til you start herdin' co-o-o-o-ows."

And on the word *cows*, he sorta drew it out into a wail that sounded like a coyote with his tail caught in a barbed-wire fence. Cow dogs usually joined in singing "cows" with him, their noses pointed at the night sky.

"That gets 'em every time," he'd say, nodding and grinning. "Them girls sure like music. Why, that's one of the things

you younger guys have to learn . . . serenadin.' You boys practice up on the guitar and go sit under a girl's window and start
serenadin' and first thing you know she's invited you in."

Well, we could see that happening, but our problem was,
how do you shut him up when he's *already* in?

Then there were the corncob pipes.

One summer, one of us read something about General
MacArthur and how he always had this corncob pipe, you see,
and then one of us bought one down at the store and got a
pouch of Half and Half and brought them both back to the
pack station. Within a week, all packers and chore boys under
the age of fifty were smoking corncob pipes. Somewhere over
the long winter, while we were separated, the corncob pipe
fetish foundered, and by the time snows had melted on the
passes and we'd returned to our bunkhouse home, nobody suggested starting that one up again.

Which was a good thing, because that was the summer of
the chipmunks, and tobacco smoke in such great quantities
couldn't be good for chipmunks.

Well, not chipmunks, really. We called them that, but tax-
onomically they were golden-mantled ground squirrels. Larger
than a true chipmunk, but still striped enough to resemble
one. Only an idiot like me would split hairs and actually look
it up and tell the others that what they were living with were
not chipmunks, which are of the family *Tamias*, but instead
were the look-alike golden-mantled ground squirrel, known
to all Latin speakers as *Spermophilus lateralis*. It is fairly easy to
tell the difference, I told them that night after my trip to the
library, because a true chipmunk has stripes on his face, and
the golden-mantled ground squirrel has instead a golden . . .
well . . . *mantle*.

"I don't care what the professor says," said one of them,
"this here's a chipmunk and calling him names is no way to
make friends with him. Ain't that right, Rat?"

At which point I think Rat bit his owner.

So two things happened that summer. We had a bunk-house full of "chipmunks" and I was called Professor until everyone scattered in the fall.

Now a chipmunk-gathering bunkhouse fetish isn't something that just happens. It has to have a beginning, and that beginning began with the boss's son, Randy Burkhart. It seems these chipmunks were invading the tack room at the pack station and pigging out on rolled barley that was intended for horses and mules. Randy, who was maybe ten that year, decided what was needed was a sure-'nuf chipmunk trapper, and he was just the guy for the job.

So he set up a box trap, sprinkled some grain under it, and waited for a chipmunk to fall for it. Before long, he had a chipmunk caught under the box, and then he discovered that both chipmunks and golden-mantled ground squirrels have teeth and know how to use them.

So he transferred his captive to a cage, sopped up the blood, and started to tame it. They tame right down, it turns out.

Randy had so much fun playing with that chipmunk that one of the guys traded him out of the thing, and took it to the bunkhouse. To keep the chipmunk from invading other people's living spaces, the owner leash broke it and tied it on about two feet of line to the leg of the bunk.

Of course, this left Randy without a chipmunk of his own, so he caught another, which was quickly traded for, and then another.

I believe, at the height of our chipmunky business, we had four of them staked out and living in the bunkhouse. Of course, even as pets they were still eating pack station grain, which did not go unnoticed at the corporate level.

Occasionally, at the end of a tension-filled day, the chipmunks would pick up on the tension and start a chatter fight with each other that only died away when the lamp was blown out.

Chipmunk season ended about a month after it began following a bunkhouse tragedy. It happened to Squeaky, the chipmunk belonging to a sixteen-year-old blond kid from the city known by the boss as Ol' Yellahair.

Ol' Yellahair and Squeaky had really become pals, and it was fun to watch them play. But one night when O.Y. was sound asleep, Squeaky climbed up the bunk's leg and crawled in with his pard for company, or maybe just to keep warm. Speculation ranged back and forth on that for a week, but we could never be certain. What we did know was that when Ol' Yellahair woke up the next morning, he found he'd rolled over and accidentally suffocated Squeaky.

Ol' Squeak looked like a miniature striped bear rug with his legs all out straight like that. Yellahair was inconsolable. The other chipmunks were released that day in a simultaneous outpouring of grief.

The rest of the summer was too busy for us to come up with any new fad, so we just moped a bit for the loss of the chipmunks and waited to see what the next summer would bring.

WHEN VARMINTS
SHOOT BACK

→

I guess I don't mind being an invader. I am, you know. So
are you, if you like the kinds of places I like. When we go
out in the woods we're invading the homes of animals,
and it's only right that we recognize it and admit it, and I'm
sure we can live with it.

We try, we always try, to leave the place neat, of course.

But when we go out there and actually live in their yard,
we can expect some invasions to turn around and head our
way. Several of these invasions have embroidered themselves
in my memory over the years.

THE RUDE GRIZZLY

When I first got to Alaska, a building contractor told me
how one night he was drinking in an Anchorage bar and met
a woman from Los Angeles who was in the Great Land to
find a husband. At a ratio of four men to every woman, this
usually isn't too difficult. She was easy on the old corneas,
to boot, so he thought he might try out for the job, or at
least enjoy himself during the interview. He bought her some
drinks and she drank them, and the evening got real cozy. It
wasn't too long before he was telling her about his beautiful

fishing cabin, which was about sixty miles away. She had to see it, and right then, and she also asked if it had a bed in it, which it did, and which prompted him to hurry out to the pickup with her in tow.

Safely settled in, with a cheery fire going in the cookstove, they were busy testing the mattress for resilience when the only door to the one-room cabin crashed open and a grizzly bear came half in the cabin.

This failure to knock had something of a serious cold-water effect on the romantic interlude, and my friend left what he was doing in a long dive, picked up the rifle, and killed the bear where it stood, half in and half out of the cabin. Despite his assurances that the bear would no longer behave rudely, she had, by this time, lost interest in mattresses, cozy cabins, Alaska and him. She had to climb over the bear's body to get out of the cabin.

My friend said that, sadly, he never saw that woman again. Sometimes romance just gets off on the wrong foot.

At Least the Moose Knocked

Everybody who lives in the woods in Alaska always keeps a loaded rifle handy. You don't go farther than the outhouse without one, and it is usually right by the door. It was that way when Pam and I were babysitting Stephan Lake Lodge that winter. I had the ought-six next to the door, and the sled dogs were chained up outside, except for Tanya's latest batch of pups, who spent a lot of time bouncing around in melting snowdrifts playing bite-my-butt, and a derivative game known to us as "Oh yeah? MAKE ME!"

It was already spring. This meant really long daylight hours, even though there was still snow on the ground and the ice was only starting to go out on the lake. We were ready for spring. Our running gin rummy scores were both over 10,000 points, and I think I still owe Pam a hundred pastrami sandwiches at David's in New York City.

So as we lay sleeping peacefully in the early morning light (about 3 a.m.) one spring day, every dog we had began throwing a fit. At my urging (she slept on the outside) she got up to see what was going on and then reported back to me along the lines of, "HE'S GOING TO KILL THE PUPPIES! AIIIIIIIEEEEE!"

Actually, nobody says *Aiiiiiieeeee*, but it's a good scream word from war comic books during the Korean Conflict and I'm going to use it here. Pam is actually more sophisticated than that. I'm using *Aiiiiiiieeeee* because her exact words accused the intruder of molesting its own mother, being born out of wedlock, cheating on a math test, and being a direct descendant of a female dog.

Well, after an *Aiiiiiiieeeee* like that one, sleep is obviously nothing but wishful history. Besides, with her leaping up and down on me yelling "Get the gun! He's going to kill the pups!" I thought I might be needed elsewhere.

I threw open the door to the cabin and there was a big bull moose, standing right there, about six feet away, facing us. His hackles were up on his back, and he was really angry, and all the dogs were screaming, and Pam was commenting on his rude qualities, and puppies were running around like ants, screaming "Mama!" at the tops of their voices.

I picked up the rifle, threw a shell in the chamber, and told the moose to go away. He didn't want to. He wanted to paw me to death, and was doing a little I-want-to-paw-him-to-death dance with his front hooves there in front of me. Now this was spring, not a good time to kill an 1800-pound seven-feet-tall bull moose. In addition to all the disrobing and subdividing I'd have to do to take care of his body, it wasn't cold enough to keep the meat, and neither of us could eat that fast.

So I shot into the gravel between his front legs. The bullet sprayed gravel all over his belly and made him jump. But after jumping, he landed in the same position again, so I hadn't really made much progress. He looked at me again, but this time he wasn't shadow boxing with those front hooves. Whatever I was, I made loud noises and he didn't like it.

"Don't make me do this," I said in as level a voice as I could muster. I thought maybe if I spoke, he'd leave. "Just go away, pal. Walk off."

I had the rifle aimed for the center of his forehead, which is as good a place as any when you're this close.

He leaned forward and I shot into the gravel again. This time he lifted his head and looked around. With all the grace and wisdom of the deer family's Mortimer Snerd–like member, he seemed to say to himself, "Well, looka here, looka here. Don't look like this is a good situation, nope, nope. Maybe I'll just mosey on down to the lake and see if there's any water in it, yup, yup. Well, so long folks. Sorry I can't stay for breakfast."

And he calmly walked off. I don't remember going back to sleep that morning.

THE WAYS OF A WOLVERINE

Wolverines are weird animals. They're the largest member of the weasel family, and the weasel family is nastier than the Borgia family ever thought of being. Wolverines, at forty pounds, have been known to tree grizzlies, and grizzlies don't tree worth a darn. I remember once during my first summer in Alaska, I asked Charlie Wolf, an old trapper from the Brooks Range, what he did when he found a wolverine in one of his traps.

"Well," he drawled, "first I empty a rifle into him. Then I come back a week later and see if he's still dead. If he is, I skin him."

In other words, a wolverine has the sense of humor of a meter maid and the warmth and love of a divorce attorney. And teeth and claws, to boot.

Down in the forest where we lived, near the Susitna River, we never saw wolverines. Oh, sometimes in winter they'd leave tracks here and there, but they just weren't really much of a factor in our lives. Until the attack on our neighbor's cabin.

Our two neighbors lived in a cabin they had just built about a mile down the river from us. We'll call them Bill and Bob, not their real names, because one of them was wanted by the law, and . . . well, it seems like the right thing to do. Bill had just returned from Vietnam (we were very busy over there at this time) and Bob had just finished a stint as an air marshal and had almost shot Elvis Presley's bodyguard at 30,000 feet.

But it was Bill who was wanted by the police. It seems the military hadn't exactly given him permission to take off his uniform and go live in the woods, and they were further upset by the fact that Bill had showed up for several months—after moving to the bush—to pick up his government paycheck. They didn't appreciate this.

That all came out much later, of course. All we knew about Bill and Bob was that they had a very real appreciation for Pam's blueberry buckle, which could charm squirrels out of the trees, and were both Olympic-class coffee drinkers.

It was winter, and they both worked quite feverishly to "get inside" and get a fire going in the stove. We had walked down there and admired their work when the cabin was finally enclosed. They were proud of it and enjoyed being out there.

One day they came over to the cabin and both of them were in shock. They had just returned from a shopping trip to Anchorage, and had found that their cabin had been thoroughly trashed. After coffee, they asked us to come look at it and see what we could make of it.

I'd never seen such a mess. That it had been done by a wolverine was plain by the tracks he left behind in the snow. The boys thought it might have been a bear, but for one thing, this was the wrong time of year, and for another, a bear can make an awful mess of a cabin, but he does it to get something to eat.

This was pure malevolence.

After ripping down and shredding their insulated plywood door, the wolverine went in and shredded their sleeping bags and dragged them to the center of the room. Then he dragged their mattresses to the center of the room and killed them. Then he shredded any and all clothing he found and dragged it to the center of the room. Not content with that, the wolverine went through the cupboards and jerked down all the canned goods, bit into each can, and added them to the pile. Then came boxes of Bisquick and cereal and tubes of toothpaste, and literally anything the guys had that they needed. When the wolverine was satisfied that he had done a pretty swell job of ruining domestic bliss for Bill and Bob, he climbed to the top of his wolverine-made pyramid and left an unmistakable pile of editorial comment on the top.

"Boys," I said, "I think you built your cabin in a wolverine's territory and he isn't happy about it."

"What should we do?"

Good question. They looked to me for advice just because I was maybe five years older than they were, and had lived in the woods a while longer. Truth was, though, I had no idea at all what to do. We consulted, Pam and I, and came up with the only suggestion that made any sense.

"All we know," I said, "is that if we leave a dog behind in camp when we take a hike, the bears will leave camp alone. I think the presence of a Chihuahua will keep bears away. But that's a bear. You might try it and see if it works on a wolverine."

So they tried it. They had to go to town and get all rigged up with household stuff again, and when they came back, we gave them some extra oak two by twelves we had that we had used for our floor in the cabin. Those planks were stout. And when they came back from town they had a half-grown big, happy Labrador retriever pup with them.

Life settled in for the guys down at Mile 238.4 and we saw them several times for coffee, blueberry buckle, and some Purina for the pooch.

Then they had to go to Anchorage for supplies again. They left the dog chained to the porch where he could guard the solid oak front door, left him plenty of dog food, and headed off down the tracks.

Upon their return the following day, they found that the wolverine had returned, torn down the oak door, destroyed the entire contents of the cabin, again, made another huge pile in the center of the cabin, and this time put the pieces of the pup on top, along with another pile of editorial comment.

That was too much. They left and we never saw them again.

THE BEST BEANS IN TOWN

When one has sled dogs, and one has groceries, one must find a way to keep them separate or all kinds of human hunger can take place. Oh, the dogs are all chained up out in the yard, with their doghouses, but escapes happen. And escapes happen as often as possible for these hairy Houdini huskies. In fact, with a few of the more skilled escape artists, we put two snaps on the end of the chain and then snapped them into the collar ring in opposite directions. A few dogs had two collars, as well. It took them quite a while to figure out they needed to develop opposable thumbs to work the snaps.

So, in the days before The Great Cabin Addition, we were living in the original twelve-foot-square log house with, as you might imagine, no storage area whatsoever. The extra groceries, then, went on the roof. We had outsmarted those huskies this time. They're clever. They're strong. But I haven't found one yet who could get into the moose meat stashed on the roof, or dive into that five-gallon can of dried beans we had up there.

Ah, yes. Five-gallon can of dried beans. That reminds me. Okay now. Remember where we left off. Moose meat, beans, roof, chained dogs, okay?

But first, this priceless quote out of the past, which I would be remiss in not sharing.

Many years ago, bush pilot and hunting guide Leon Shellabarger, of Skwentna, was loading a young couple into his plane to fly them to camp. The woman saw his five-gallon can of dried beans in the back of the plane and asked about them.

"That's my emergency food," he explained. "You know, just in case."

"But Mr. Shellabarger," she said, "you have pinto beans and kidney beans and lima beans all mixed together in that can."

He smiled at her. "Honey, if I ever have to open that can, I'll have plenty of time to sort 'em."

I didn't think you'd mind that short detour.

But back at the home place at Trinity Creeks. Food on roof, fire in stove, dogs on chain, God's in his heaven, all's right with the world.

Until early one summer morning, full daylight, when the dogs are going stark-staring nuts at full volume. It seems like it took me forever to get Pam up to go check on it, too. She told me to get up, then, because she wasn't sure what was going on.

So I got dressed and grabbed The Mooser (the .30–06) and stepped outside. All the dogs were barking furiously and were looking toward the cabin roof, so I set the rifle down and climbed up the corner of the cabin where the log overlaps make a dandy ladder. As I stuck my head over the top of the roof, I said hello to Mrs. Black Bear and her two youngsters, Binky and Dum-Dum, who were enjoying a raw bean repast, mixed with raw flour, at our expense. Mama and I were about three feet apart, nose-to-nose measurement, and I suddenly remembered I'd forgotten to leave something down on the porch.

Me.

I grabbed the rifle, ducked back inside the cabin, stuck the barrel out into the sky and popped off a round. The three bears then decided to leave this noisy place and try Goldilocks again.

It rained hard later that day. In fact, it rained hard before we had a chance to do any cleaning up on that roof. But being of a scientific bent, we learned that when a paste of raw beans and raw flour dries, it becomes a roof that looks like a freckled ghost, but one that is blessedly impervious to extreme weather.

Every dark cloud, etc.

SHOW MERCY, YOUR HONOR

About a month before our daughter Mandy was born, we took the dogs and moved to Anchorage for the duration. This was in the late fall of 1973. We stayed with friends and I found work in an insulation factory, which consisted of stapling my fingers to sheets of roofing.

When Mandy was about three weeks old (this would be just before Christmas), we loaded her on the sled and headed back for the cabin. But things had changed some since we'd left. We'd left big containers of dog food and people food in the cabin (since we took the sled dogs with us, we didn't have to put the stuff on the roof) including a big sack of cornmeal. We cooked that cornmeal to make the dog food last longer. Little did we know that cornmeal is a legendary basic food group for red squirrels everywhere, and one of them had moved in.

This was a monster squirrel. This bad boy was a Boone and Crockett record-book red squirrel. For two months he'd had free reign of the cabin and its delights, including all the cornmeal a guy could ask for. The problem was, when we left the cabin, the fire went out in the stove. It was cold in there, and no squirrel likes a cold cabin with his cold cuts, so he solved the problem by ripping out the pink insulation we'd used to chink between the logs and had built himself a House Beautiful nest under the kitchen table. He was only able to reach up about two logs' worth, of course, as red squirrels, even when fed cornmeal free choice, simply aren't that tall.

There he was, sitting there like the Laughing Buddha in his rolls of fat, lounging in his Owens Corning pleasure palace, telling us we'd have to find another place to live because he still had the best part of twenty-two pounds of cornmeal left in the sack. Most red squirrels say "chip, chip." Not our guy. In a cornmeal-enhanced basso, he said "*CHURP! CHURP!*"

And it rattled the coffee cups.

Well, out he went at the business end of Pam's broom, and we soon had the squirrel nest disassembled and stuffed back between the logs. We got a fire going in the stove, and in another hour or so, the frost had lifted enough from the logs that we could open the bundle of blankets to let Amanda Lois Randles have her first look at her home.

We had a loft built for sleeping at this time, and we took the baby to bed with us. It was good that we did, too, because in the middle of the night, here came Pancho Villa, the bandit red squirrel, back for more. We woke up with our noses covered in frost, and wondered why the stove was failing us. Well, when all the insulation is pulled out of two horizontal log layers, and when said insulation is again piled into a Casa de Squirrel under the kitchen table, things cool right down. At this point I could picture three lonely headstones sitting under a tree, with one simple epitaph: "Frozen to Death by a Well-Fed Squirrel."

That was when I discovered that Pam's Berkeley-graduate-enhanced attitude of live-and-let-live and cosmic karma and infinite justice could be suspended when it came to having a baby in the cabin.

"Death!" yelled the prosecuting attorney.

"Death!" yelled the jury.

"Death!" agreed the judge.

Strangely, all these folks resembled Mandy's mom.

So the sentence was carried out. The cabin became warm again, the groceries were returned to their rightful owners, and life with the new baby went on. But the squirrel might have had the last laugh as he rolled in our cornmeal one final time.

PAM'S EARRINGS

There are people who have lived in Alaska's Bush for forty years and more who have never had to use a rifle to protect themselves. I've known quite a few. We weren't that lucky. And it's because some people aren't that lucky that every cabin dweller and prospector and logger is armed.

Our problem arose in the first couple of days we were on our new property north of Talkeetna. No cabin there yet, of course. No trail, even. We filed on the five acres under the state's open-to-entry land program. It wasn't homesteading. Homesteading is for farmers, and there has to be land clearing, house building, residency requirements, all that stuff. Plus, homesteading is a federal program and is for 160 acres. There's very little, if any, of that going on any more.

But the open-to-entry land program says you have to go out and put the corner posts in yourself, but that's all it requires. You don't even have to go back to it again. They'd let you rent the land for $40 a year until you could afford to pay for a survey. Once the survey was done, you could buy the land from the state for $500. This was a fairly short-lived program, and was open only in areas far from roads, but it was really popular. I think you had five years to pony up that $500, so this was a way literally anyone could afford a home of their own.

With us, this wasn't a weekend project. When we filed on the land, we moved there. I was a columnist at this point for *The Anchorage Daily News*, and lest you equate that with wealth and fame, I'll just explain that this gave us a steady income of ten bucks a week. As for the fame part, this meant that, occasionally, someone on the train would recognize me from my mug shot being in the paper and say something to the effect of, "You that guy from the paper, ain't ya? Well, when you've been here as long as I have, you'll know what you're talking about."

Pam had left her full-time job waiting tables in Girdwood at the ski resort to run off to the woods with dogs and a crazy man and, as one friend put it, "carve a civilization out of the wilderness."

We embarked on this adventure in June of 1971, and just to find our property, which sits on a little creek about a quarter mile through six-feet-tall bluejoint grass (sweetgrass) and Devil's Club from the railroad tracks, required the liberal use of a machete. For the record, we had a couple of sleeping bags, two old Sears camping tents that held back everything but bears and rain, forty dollars in cash and an income of forty dollars a month, a True Temper Hudson's Bay ax (no saw), about forty feet of rope, a bucket of log spikes a friend had given us, a borrowed .30–06, and four or five sled dogs. Is this the way to do it? Of course not.

I remember sometime later in the summer, when we could afford to buy a Swede saw (also called a bow saw) for about ten dollars, how rich we felt at the time. A chainsaw was something one could only dream of in those days.

Pam cooked our meals over an open campfire there in front of the tents, and it rained all the time. Quite an adventure.

You know what an adventure is, right? An adventure occurs when you haven't planned properly.

We had all the ingredients necessary to make a successful pioneer couple, as Pam was from a suburb of San Francisco and I was from a suburb of Los Angeles. And we both survived.

"You know not to build out of anything but spruce, right?" said our aged pal, Rocky Cummings in Talkeetna. "And build up above where them cottonwoods are. Where a cottonwood tree is, it floods there."

"And don't build out of cottonwood, whatever you do," chimed in Rocky's partner, Jim Beaver. "You know why? Because a twelve-inch cottonwood log will shrink an inch a year for thirteen years."

It's always nice to provide old sourdoughs with entertainment, you know? And we did appreciate the advice.

As someone who has attempted to commit journalism for more than forty years now, I not only treasured both these guys for their friendship, but I also treasured Rocky (in his eighties at the time) for giving a pal of mine from an Anchorage radio station the shortest radio interview in history.

"So Rocky," said the interviewer, "how long have you lived in Talkeetna?"

Rocky thought a second. "I guess about fifty years now."

"Wow! Fifty years! I guess you've seen a lot of changes around here in that time."

"Well . . . no."

So there we were, in our soggy tents, by a soggy pile of firewood, on our second or third soggy day there. We were feeling . . . soggy. Naturally, we decided to take time off from being soggy and go fishing. We took the rifle, naturally, and the dogs, and probably had fun. We always did. When we returned, it was to find that bears had been through our stuff, knocked down both tents, trashed everything, and we saw the butt end of one of the black bears heading off through the forest.

What a mess. We started going through our stuff, feeling much like flood or hurricane or tornado victims. One of the bears, we discovered, wasn't too fussy about what he ate. On his menu that day was one 35mm roll of color film, a plastic lemon full of lemon juice (including the plastic lemon itself), a pouch of Sir Walter Raleigh pipe tobacco, and a can of Sterno. This last consists largely of Napalm and Vaseline, I think. He'd licked it clean. And so this led me to leave Pam in camp cleaning up the mess while I took the rifle and prowled out into the grass, knowing for a fact that there was a bear dying of indigestion out there. Had to be.

The first thing I heard, however, was Pam screaming "There's another one!" I ran back to camp just in time to see a black bear heading for Pam at a full run. Before I had a chance to act, our lead dog, A-Bob (named for the Arkansas cousin of the guy who gave him to us) slammed head-on into that 300-pound bear and rolled him. When the bear recovered and started for Pam again, I killed him.

That deadly interlude at what we later named Trinity Creeks dedicated the place for us. The place was blooded, and thankfully it wasn't our blood. From that moment on, the place was home. We had too much invested in it by that time to think of it any other way.

Pam fashioned a pair of earrings out of the bear's canine teeth, and they were quite spectacular, as the tooth root is about three-quarters of the length of the whole tooth, so it looked more like something from a Tyrannosaurus by the time she finished.

That isn't the end of the story of the bear earrings, though.

A couple of years later, we went down to Pam's home town of Palo Alto, California. This is also the home of Stanford University, of course, and the tower designed by former President Herbert Hoover, known locally as "Hoover's Last Erection." It is also the locale of Cubberley High School, famous for educating Joan Baez's little sister, and Pam. It was time for her tenth high school reunion, and we went.

She wore the earrings.

I had felt, at the ripe old age of twenty-nine, as though I were still a young man just starting out in life. But then I went to this reunion and started feeling old. Here were a bunch of guys twenty-seven years old, fat and balding, standing around comparing retirement plans. *Retirement plans!*

"Hey, Bobby! Whatcha been up to?"

"Hello there, Pete. Well, well, the years have certainly been kind to you. Well, Martha and me have had some wild times, I can tell you. You know the cat got all excited, back in October, and threw up on the carpet."

"You don't say? How'd you get it cleaned up?"

"Well, Martha found this new cleaning stuff down at the mall . . ."

Then one of the ladies would notice Pam's earrings and ask about them. . . .

Hey, sometimes those reunions can be fun.

A RETURN TO THE SADDLE
FICTION

———————————————————————————————▶

Those first days were sore days. Slow days. Remembering days. We'd move the pickets to put Chuckles and Duster on fat grass, and we'd water them often. But mostly we sat and talked . . . of old days and good things and maybe just a touch or two of friendly slander.

But every day we rode. At first we rode only an hour or two and then spent the rest of the day stretching and moving slowly and asking ourselves questions about sanity.

Smokey recovered in about four days, but it took me more than a week. Maybe it was two weeks. We weren't counting by then. City life plays dirty tricks on a cowboy. The body that was once tuned to a horse now sat astride with a stupid expression asking, "Just what the hell is this you expect me to do?"

But Chuckles was a gentle, patient partner. As we'd lope off across the sagebrush, he forgave the floppiness and miscues as we grew to learn each other. Chuckles lost his grass belly and got back into shape before I did. He breathed more easily on our daily lopes over the hills. In a short time, he'd tuned himself into a running machine.

And as my muscles and mind gradually switched over to horseback, I really began to appreciate this bay horse. I'd never ridden a horse that was as smooth through rock piles and the sage flats. He flowed over and around obstacles. And, to my everlasting shock, about a week or so later, I began to flow with him.

What happens is inexplicable and deserves a few moments' consideration. There is a memory built into the mind and the muscles that, once learned, never disappears. There comes a moment that good horsemen learn, when you cease being man and horse and become a traveling unit. When it happens, it is a wondrous thing. You can sit back and remember the feeling again and again in later years when all you ride is a pickup truck.

You learn the way the horse thinks and how he moves, and how far each leg moves on each stride and just where he'll put his feet. And a lot of it depends on how long his legs are and how flat or steep the terrain may be. You can look down, in the early stages, and know just where the right hoof will go and where the left hoof will go. Just ahead of that rock with the right, and just short of that clump of grass with the left. And later in this early stage, you'll begin to know by feel where those hind legs are going to touch down. And when those massive hindquarters give a heave up over a log, you are with him and you know it. Because you *know* it.

Then, after many hours in the saddle over long days, and if you have spent years riding in your youth, you can pick up once again the rhythm of the horse. Not just any horse, but this nice bay, Chuckles. No two horses will run a dodging pattern through sagebrush the same. It may look the same to someone who is watching, but not to the rider in the saddle. Each horse's way of traveling is like a fingerprint. Blindfolded, and at any gait, you will be able to tell your horse from others.

Finally, your unstretched muscles limber up and begin to fit the saddle and the horse. As this happens, you can begin to feel the horse beneath you as an extension of yourself and not an alien being whose back you are on for transportation.

Finally, when the horse is let out into a run, your muscles flex along and you sense, rather than see, the changes in the ground beneath you. When the horse strains over an obstacle, your body strains with it, shifting to put your body where it will do the horse the most good. And these reflexes happen ten times to a second, twenty or fifty times to a second, until there is just one being with two brains moving through the brush, with one brain telegraphing movement to the other, and the other sending body signals to the first. And one says where you'll go, and the other says how you'll go, and the two just go and flow, like some primordial fugue, with the messages chasing each other and complementing each other and all of it making sense and a spooky kind of poetry at the same time.

That's what happens when it's good.

We rode that way, looking over the country for a week and more than a week. We watched the wild horses, although we knew we didn't have to. And we scouted the country and looked in old abandoned mines and killed a few snakes. And twice we ducked into deep ravines when we heard the scream of the jets, and then we came out again.

One day, while riding alone, I stopped up on a ridge where I could see the Sierra peaks, and I stepped off and sat on a rock and just watched the peaks. Sometimes it helped.

See those peaks? Nothing you will do in your lifetime will affect them. Nothing anyone has done in millions of lifetimes has affected them. Your personal problems are no more to them than the burrow of a marmot in one of their myriad rockslides. Less than that. Whether I have a happy life, or a short life, or a miserable life, or no life at all won't change this particular view. Ever.

We may be less than nothing, but we have dreams, and dreams are something rocks and peaks are denied.

During these days, the hardest work was fixing up the old mustanger's corral about three miles from camp. Wind and neglect had knocked most of it down, and that sometimes meant riding a great distance to find dead branches to strengthen it.

The only good thing about fixing up that old corral was feeling the difference in our muscles as the days went by, gradually getting warmer as the sun pushed along toward the inevitable blast that is summer.

There was something else happening, too. There comes a nice feeling one day when you swing up into the saddle more easily, because either you don't weigh as much as you did, or you're just stronger than you were, and it doesn't matter a damn which. Then, too, old forgotten smells and textures return. Your boots become used to the weight of the large, gentle California spurs, and your ears pick up the familiar chiming of the rowels as you walk. The chaps take on that particular hang they used to have until it feels right for you to have them on and just a little bit naked when you take them off. Your hat has always fit right.

It was good relearning the smells, too. Like the honest sweat of work in the sun. It came to have a familiar feel to it, and I discovered I wasn't running to the falls to wash twice a day. Even if I ate with dusty hands, no undue poisoning occurred. In fact, I realized I felt pretty good.

And as the days went along, I began to notice the texture of the mountains around me and thought less and less of the news that was undoubtedly taking place all over the world.

Somewhere out there, banks were being robbed and babies were born and terrorists were killing people and governments were forming and toppling, and none of them required my immediate attention. I hadn't taken a pill in a long time, now, and began to wonder why I ever had.

I rode hard enough during the day now that I dropped to sleep almost immediately after pulling off my boots and sliding into the chilly bedroll. About the time my own body heat made the bedroll warm enough to unclench my muscles, my mind unclenched as well until morning. I didn't want to think.

It had to be enough, right then, to let the mountains become part of me and shape me back into a child of its wild canyons. The fine dust of the alkali flats began to coat things with its graphitic touch and make my chaps polish my saddle and my saddle polish my chaps.

Everything seemed to fit. One lazy afternoon we'd been out looking over a small valley full of horses and taking turns watching the flying-saucer-shaped Sierra wave clouds twist themselves into stratospheric ghosts. When the coolness of the late afternoon came, we silently got on our horses and rode back toward camp. It had to be a good three miles back, and suddenly Smokey put the spurs to Duster and the sabino flew like a bat through the sagebrush. Chuckles wanted to run, so I let him, and we were sailing along through occasional war whoops down the long, gentle ridge swells toward camp.

Duster went wide around a rock pile and Chuckles flew over it and made up the difference, and then we were side by side racing along, the horses breathing easily and straining good-naturedly in the race.

I looked across at Smokey and we grinned at each other and yelled a few more times, and then we were quiet, just flowing with the pounding run of our horses and watching the sage get sucked up beneath those churning pistons.

It seemed, too, with the frantic pounding of the hooves, that the mountain picked up the counterpoint and gave us some music to listen to with a silent inner ear. It wasn't the flash and fire of Rossini, but the soft morning music of the Impressionists. Debussy in the desert, Ravel through the ravines. It was a haunting song born of the earth and the mountain and wild things and it swelled up slowly to that hidden ear and soothed in contrast to the heavy pace of the running horses. It was the kind of song that makes a man think perhaps he's losing his mind just a little, but it's so pretty he doesn't care. I had heard it before, but not for a long time.

It ended when I pulled Chuckles up just short of camp, and watched as Smokey and Duster went skittering through the camp, jumping the fire pit and then sliding to a stop beyond.

We walked the horses together down an arroyo to let them blow; then I took Duster's reins so Smokey could rustle us up a dinner fire.

"Pard?" I said.

"Yeah?"

"I've got my seat back."

"Aw hell, Buck." He grinned. "Never thought you'd lost it."

THINK BEFORE
YOU STINK

⟶

*H*ey, *what good would a book on the outdoors be without a little how-to thrown in? So here's something from my how-to book on hunting elk.*

Our hunting industry is nothing if not clever. We come up with forty-'leven kinds of camouflage when all we need is one. We come up with scents that attract, repel, or offend both the elk and our neighbors.

Why? For the same reason people tie fancy, colorful fishing flies. Fish don't buy them; fishermen buy them. Experienced fishermen have known for some time that fish eat ugly brown bugs. Fish actually prefer these over the gorgeous flashy flies that resemble no bug ever born and are given names like Sequined Hollywood Hooker.

Hunters often want to know if they should spray themselves with cow elk urine so the bull will think they're in heat, and I don't know the answer to that one, because it's against the law to use an attractant lure here in New Mexico. We just don't get any practice with that stuff.

But there are always those so-called cover scents that are sold by the expensive ounce on every other page of every outdoor magazine in the world. For $4.95 down at Mega-Mart, you can buy scents in plastic bubble packs that will make you smell like a fox, a skunk, a tree, or (my favorite) an apple.

The object, of course, is that an elk won't smell sweaty stinking man stuff, but will be lulled into lassitude by something that smells like an apple tree as he walks along at 9,000 feet in the spruce forest.

Come on! Let's think a minute. What is it we want?

• With the exception of the peak of the rut, when we want Ol' Hat Rack to think we're another bull, we want him to think we aren't even there.

We want to move through the mountains invisibly. We don't want to call attention to ourselves. That's why we take such pains to watch wind direction and walk so slowly that we don't crunch leaves or crack twigs.

So why should we smell like an apple?

Or a skunk or a fox or a raccoon or a '59 Oldsmobile or whatever squirt bottle we carry in our jacket pocket?

There you are on a stand overlooking this nice little meadow that is picture perfect except it needs a bull in the middle of it. Along comes the bull, sticks his head out into the open and he catches a whiff of—not man, mind you—but fox. Do you really think he isn't going to take a few seconds and look for the fox? Of course he will. A fox is no threat to him, but a fox (or skunk or squirrel or kid's tricycle) is part of what's around him. He's lived this long by checking things out.

• If you smell like a fox, he will look up the hill and check you out.

Is that what you want?
Not me.

• I want to smell like nothing. *Nothing.*

I want to be as close to invisible as I can. Since in almost every hunting situation, success depends on seeing the bull before the bull sees you, I don't want to smell like anything.

A Little Story #1
During the peak of the rut, which usually falls in late bow season, it doesn't hurt to smell like a rutting bull. The best elk hunter I know, Bill Clark, likes to find an elk wallow, give a war whoop, and flop himself down in it and roll around. You don't want to know how an elk prepares a wallow. I had to share a tent with Bill.
Did I mention he was single?

Then there's the question of clothing.

There are a couple of spray-on deodorants for clothes, and I have a big expensive bottle of it in the pantry someplace. It's good stuff. Doesn't hurt. I must admit I almost never use it, but it seems to be a good product.

There's a much cheaper way of doing the same thing.

The secret takes place in the washing machine. When the rinse cycle comes along, I stop the machine.

- Instead of putting "Panties So Soft and Sweet" softener in the water, I dump in a handful of baking soda. I usually let the stuff sit for five or ten minutes before resuming the action.

Really does the job. That stuff eats stink.

There are other things you can do, too. If you want to be a purist about it (which I recommend strongly for bow hunters, where propinquity is the order of the day) you can remove your hunting clothes the minute you are back in camp and seal them in a plastic bag. The most important part of this, of course, is to remember to put some other clothes on before asking the cook if there is any coffee.

There's nothing wrong with a little cover scent when you do this, either, but you have to use your head about it.

- If you want your clothes to smell like something other than clothes, or you, go grab a sprig of spruce and stick it in there.

If you are hunting southern mountains, like the Gila, a sprig of sage works well. A handful of baking soda in the bag is always good.

- But if you use a sprig of something, for Pete's sake pick something that actually lives where you hunt.

Are all these steps necessary? Probably not. But one or two of these things could boost your chances at taking an elk way up, way, way up.

Don't let him know you are there.

For the record, bull elk consider tobacco smoke to be foreign to them. Strange as it may seem, they associate tobacco smoke with hunters and shy away from it.

- Do not go to all the trouble of deodorizing yourself and your clothes and your rifle or bow and your backpack and then get into the cab of a pickup and light one up.

And if your guide smokes, ask him to wait a while, or climb over the tailgate and ride in the back.

Common sense about common scents, that's all. Think before you stink.

TIP:

If you forget to bring the whetstone to camp with you, find two small pieces of slate, wet them and rub them together. They'll smooth each other out and you'll get two whetstones that will put an edge on that knife.

OLD INDIAN TRICK NUMBER ONE

It was Bill Clark who introduced me to one of the best elk-hunting secrets I know: alfalfa pills. You can buy these harmless tablets for a couple of cents each down at the supermarket or at any health food store. They're supposed to have some health benefits, like making your nose twitch like a rabbit or something, but the only important thing is, they eliminate human odor.

Let me repeat that:

• They eliminate human odor.

If you have questions about their safety, ask your doctor, but I checked with mine (I have some pills to take, too) and he said no sweat. (No pun intended this time.)

So if you check out okay, here's what you do. Take two tablets with each meal three days before you start your hunt. If you are like I am with math, that means six tablets a day. Continue taking them throughout the hunt. Period. That's all there is to it.

A Little Story #2
Bill told me about alfalfa pills years ago and I decided to give them a try during a bow hunt in the Gila. There I was, dressed like a pile of leaves and full of alfalfa, and I leaned back against a log, closed my eyes for a second, and fell asleep. When I awoke, it was to stare into the face of a mule deer doe at a range of 10 feet. She was staring at me, stomping her front feet, and making little snorts. A yearling and twin fawns were about twenty feet away. The wind was brushing the back of my neck and blowing straight to her.

• Now she knew I was something, but she didn't know what.

I lay there for maybe thirty seconds, just watching her and wondering when she would catch on to what I was.

She didn't. Finally, I had to move, so I smiled and said. "Good morning. ma'am," and away they all flew.

I became a believer in alfalfa pills right then and there. On that same hunt, which is in early September in southern New Mexico—this translates to climbing steep mountains in 90 degree heat—I returned home dripping sweat after a week without a bath, and my wife couldn't smell me. I even got a hug. This from a woman who can smell a ham sandwich that's gone questionable in a closed refrigerator in someone else's house down the street.

Oh man, do they work!

TIP:

To make it back to camp before sundown, hold your hand out at arm's length between you and the late afternoon sun. Every finger width between the sun and the horizon means fifteen minutes before sundown. Four fingers is an hour, etc.

—from *Dancing Through Dark Timber:
A Commonsense Approach to Elk Hunting*

MANDY'S FIRST SALMON

→

There aren't too many fishermen who remember catching their first fish, because so many of us come from outdoor families that we were fishing before we were remembering. Now I remember my first fish because I didn't come from a fishing family, and I caught it (well, transferred it, actually) the summer I turned eleven, at a campground near Fallen Leaf Lake, near Lake Tahoe.

A black water snake had already caught this six-inch trout, and I caught the snake and took the fish away from him. We ate it. He was really upset. After that, I talked my dad into letting me get some fishing tackle to pursue the sport in a more orthodox fashion.

But the "first fish" I remember best was my daughter Mandy's.

Her radio listening public knows her as Amanda Randles these days, but for her family members, she'll always be Mandy, the redheaded terror of Alaska's tall timber. Well, I'm lying. She's really nice.

Mandy was born in Anchorage, and Pam and I took her home to the cabin by dog team when she was about three weeks old. She's been what Alaskans refer to as a "skookum chick" ever since. She was helping pack in stovewood from outside when she was just barely old enough to walk. She lived miles from a road and seemed to be one of the happiest youngsters anyone has ever seen. She started straightening out sled dogs by admonishing them and calling them the most demeaning thing a toddler going through potty training could think of: "Stop it! You . . . you PAMPERS!"

When Mandy was three, Pam and I started a weekly newspaper and went from living twelve miles north of Talkeetna to eleven miles south of Talkeetna. In a rented cabin there, we had electricity and pavement and were more mobile. We still didn't have a phone, but through a CB radio and local gossip, we were able to come up with a newspaper each week.

That summer, Jim and Cathy Kershner, our very close friends, were teaching their three kids to fish. The kids were older than Mandy, and she wanted very much to learn, too. This last clause is one of the great understatements of this modest book. Let's just say this redheaded three year old was determined to begin fishing.

Now her mother, Pam, is one of the great fly fishermen of the world, and was more than ready to teach her. As was I. Pam, another redhead (where do they come from?) has an interesting approach to fishing. She believes that only certain fish are worth catching. Those fish are the ones with good taste enough to bite down on a Royal Coachman fly, because a Royal Coachman is pretty. Lest you laugh, amigos and amigettes, let me add here that Pam has caught fish with a Royal Coachman where experienced fishermen were getting skunked with more conventional methods. Nor does Pam insist on the Royal Coachman being a dry fly. Spies tell me she once amazed the village of Shageluk, where she was teaching school, by going out at lunchtime and catching fish with a Royal Coachman through a hole in the ice.

Is this an intelligent way to fish? Well, maybe not to everyone else, but to Pam, it made sense. Why mess with stupid fish who have no sense of beauty, symmetry, or art?

How tasty could some stupid fish be who'd eat a worm, for crying out loud?

Pam, of course, is a college graduate. The first night we met, in Girdwood, Alaska, she told me she'd graduated from the University of California at Berkeley.

"Great," I said. "What years did you go there?"

"I was there from the Free Speech Movement to People's Park," she said.

I didn't need to ask what she did after class let out.

She proudly told me for years that the FBI had a file on her and she considered herself to be a serious threat to such things as the Nixon Administration, the free enterprise system, and the conservative movement. We had very interesting dinner-table conversations.

When the Freedom of Information Act was passed, we were able to learn the contents of her FBI file. Three words. "Noisy but harmless."

She was outraged.

Outraged, but laughing at the same time.

So this was the background for three-year-old Mandy Randles becoming a danger to the greater salmon population of Alaska. After her wheedling had wheedled us down, we bought her a Zebco spinning outfit for little kids. You know the one. Glass rod about three feet long with a closed-face spinning reel on it. To play it safe, I picked up one of those rubber plugs so she could practice casting without killing anyone. We told her if she could cast that safely, and could handle it without beaning someone with that rubber plug, we would take her fishing.

No one ever cast a rubber plug more enthusiastically over the next few days. In an hour or two, she got to where she could cast without creaming some dog or cat or mother. Then she went for the accuracy part of it, and was finally able to look around her, make sure no one was within range, cast her rubber plug a full eight feet in front of her, and reel it back in properly. She was ready for the big time.

So one day Jim and I gathered up the four kids and went down to Sheep Creek, where there was a run of humpies (pink salmon) taking place. A big humpy will weigh maybe four pounds, so it wasn't like Ahab going after Moby Dick here, and there was an excellent chance Jim's kids could catch a couple. And Mandy? Well, she had the same chance as the others, but casting only eight feet was considered something of a fishing handicap in those days. It still is. Except in ice fishing.

Now a girl can't catch a salmon with a rubber plug (which I'd been told more than several times at that point) so I tied on a red and white salmon spoon, just like the other kids had.

I told her to be really careful and to fish away from the others a little for safety's sake. No fisherman was ever more serious than she was. She was well aware of those sharp treble hooks and watched very carefully where they were at all times. She'd stand on the bank and cast that spoon. Sometimes it would even hit the water.

Satisfied that my daughter was safely occupied in trying to reach the water with that lure, I turned to help one of Jim's kids untangle some line. I wasn't prepared for the screaming of the line going out through those Zebco rod guides and the loud whirring of the reel. We turned and looked, and there went Mandy into Sheep Creek (which is the size of a river, you understand) with her rod bent nearly double and the most determined look on her face. She'd hooked a good one, and he was taking her out to sea.

I jumped in the creek and snatched her up in my arms just about the time the water reached her armpits. She wouldn't let go of the rod, so I carried her back to solid ground and she dragged a salmon along with her. And just before I set her down on the ground, she looked at me with a furious red face and said, "Daddy! That's *my* fish!"

Oh Lord! Another one in the family.

A Horse Called
Tornado

———————————————————➤

He might have been the worst roping horse in California. It's hard to be certain, because back in those days they didn't have competitions to see who the worst is. People in those days were trying to be the best.

But although he wouldn't work a rope, and there were Brahma calves that could outrun him, he was my horse.

The summer I turned fourteen, I got a job at Stanley Ranch in the hills north of Los Angeles. This was a Woodcraft Rangers boys' camp, and I'm a third generation Ranger myself. I was a dishwasher. A mighty dishwasher. No one scrubbed pots harder than I did. I alternated exercising this talent with putting pitchers of "bug juice" (Kool-Aid) on the tables for the campers faster than the speed of light.

The camp had horses, and everyone got to ride. Of course, I was mere staff, so I had to get some riding in whenever I could sneak away, and the nice part was I didn't have to go out as part of a "ride" which was accompanied by someone who knew what he was doing.

And on my sneak rides, I kinda partnered up with a very skinny bay gelding named Two Bits. They didn't want him there, and no one else rode him, because he'd "behaved badly" a time or two and kids who were riding him and goofing off found themselves sitting in the dirt and wondering what happened.

At this point, I surely wasn't a cowboy, just a skinny 100-pound kid with glasses, but I'd learned riding from my Uncle Roy, who lived two doors away and had a horse. So I'd been riding something since I was about four. When I was nine, I had a donkey named Jenny and we spent many happy hours with her scraping me and my younger brothers off under a convenient apricot tree limb.

So Two Bits and I got along all right. We had a pact; I didn't do stupid things on him and he didn't buck me off.

I'd saved my dishwashing money, and when my stint behind the scrub brush was over, I'd managed to buy Two Bits for fifty bucks.

The camp director told me they called him Two Bits 'cause he was a Quarter Horse. Others thought this might have reflected his actual value. From the way they looked at each other, I thought his old name was probably more attuned to his standing on the stock exchange, so I changed it.

You see, when you have a starve-to-death boys-camp reject horse coupled with a skinny nearsighted fourteen-year-old kid, you have real possibilities. Together they will undoubtedly ride the range together, fashioning ranches out of mere desert, building civilizations wherever they go, rescuing damsels, tilting at evil black knights. A year later, by popular acclaim (which means I insisted on it) I began to be known as Slim. So when we first partnered up, it was a pact between Tony and Two Bits. But my horse changed his name first. His name, I proudly told the family when we got him to his backyard corral there in El Monte, was Tornado. Now *there's* a name! The world would soon see that a combo known as Slim and Tornado could do things that Tony and Two Bits could never have accomplished.

We were a match when it came to skinny. My dad used to tell people we had to feed this horse around the clock to keep the buzzards from circling the house.

My life in those days began every afternoon about three when Tornado and I saddled up and hit the trail down the cement channel that used to be the Rio Hondo, about a block from home.

We'd ride through subdivisions and under concrete and steel bridges and go past the backs of industrial parks smelling of chemicals and sounding like saws cutting through steel. But in reality, the reality that belonged solely to Slim and Tornado, we were gliding through alpine meadows, chasing wild horses across the tops of New Mexico's mesas, and galloping toward the castle to vanquish whatever varlets were threatening the lady fair. In fact, every morning since I got that horse, I'd been doing push-ups just so I'd be ready for varlet vanquishing when the need arose. I could do seven or eight on a good day.

Tornado not only filled my afternoons with fun and my days with dreams, but he defined me. I wore cowboy boots to high school. I did everything cowboy that I could get away with. I bought a rope and began roping buckets. Somewhere in the family archives is a snapshot of me mowing the lawn with a piggin' string in my teeth.

I befriended a professional calf roper named Dick Johnson, who had a grazing lease on 1100 acres of oil fields about five miles from my home, down the riverbed. He had a practice arena and some calves, and he always needed someone to open the chutes and untie calves and help feed the stock in the evenings. So that was where Tornado and I went each afternoon.

Dick was a wonderful guy, and let me learn roping there when he wasn't too busy. He was also a good sounding board for any dreams I had, even if he might have been a bit too brutally honest.

I recall one time in the stock truck when he asked me what I wanted to do when I grew up. I said I wanted to be a singer.

"Okay," he said. "Let's hear you sing something."

So, in my best Sinatra imitation, I started in on "Everybody Loves Somebody."

When I finished, he looked at me and smiled, and said. "I think you ought to be a lawyer, like your dad."

Not me. I knew all about lawyering. Lawyering meant going to school, even after you *had* to go to school. And lawyering meant driving into a big city and going to the eleventh floor of the A. P. Giannini Building in Los Angeles. Not me. I hated school. For me, school was something you did while you waited to get old enough to live. The only thing I was good at in school was writing. When I was a freshman there at Rosemead High School, I wrote a short story for class about a roping horse. The teacher submitted it for publication in the high school literary magazine called *Penopsis* and that was my first published work. The piece was called "Money Horse," and I mention it only because they had one of the seniors do an illustration for it. His name was Bob Mackie and he went on to become a world-famous dress designer.

Horses dragged me further into writing about a year later. My mother wrote a chatty neighborhood column for the local paper. I kept urging her to write about my pal, Dick Johnson.

"Mom!" I said. "This guy is a professional rodeo hand and has an 1100-acre cattle ranch in the middle of Los Angeles!"

Even then I could smell a good story.

"Well," she said, "why don't you talk to Dick and write a little story about him and we'll see what we can do with it?"

So I cornered Dick and learned about his past and asked him some really dumb questions which I blissfully can't remember at all, and I borrowed an action photo of him roping at the L.A. Coliseum, and went home and wrote a little story. I was hoping Mom would put it in her own words and run it in her column.

Instead, they ran it as a feature story with my byline on it, with a two-column photo of Dick roping, and they asked me to write a column on cowboys every week. We called it "Chutin' the Bull," and it ran for about a year and a half until I escaped.

I went to rodeos and interviewed everyone who knew more about rodeo than I did, which was everyone.

I remember going to cover the L.A. Coliseum rodeo once. I took Tornado, of course. Didn't need a pass or a ticket. When I pulled up to the contestants' gate towing a horse trailer, the guy just waved me on in. When I rode Tornado through the tunnel and into the coliseum, they figured if I was on a horse in the middle of Los Angeles, I probably belonged there, and waved me on in. That was the day I interviewed Jim Shoulders, a great world champion rodeo cowboy, one of my idols.

I found Jim stretched out in the shade of the ambulance there before the rodeo began. So I took out my notebook and squirmed under the ambulance to interview him, there beneath the differential.

But how to start the interview? I mean, this was JIM SHOULDERS!

Over the years, I've interviewed many sports greats, including Joe DiMaggio, but this was JIM SHOULDERS!

So I poised myself with the pencil and waited until Jim turned his head and looked at me. I smiled.

"Sure is cool down here," I said, stupidly.

"Beats being in the thing," he said.

I wrote that down, of course.

So the column itself was a success. They paid me fifteen cents a column inch, which bought Tornado's hay, and they gave me a press pass, which meant I didn't have to pay to get into any rodeo anywhere. After spending more than forty years full time in journalism, that still seems to be the best use for a press pass.

Although I lived for the afternoons and weekends when Tornado and I could chase calves and maybe catch one now and then, I was still plagued by school. Besides writing "Money Horse," there was one other little dealie I wrote for English class as a sophomore which drew some attention.

We were to write some *poetry verité*, which I took to mean telling the truth. So I wrote this little *verité*:

Two strong arms, a fine mind, and youth
All in vain.
Outside of class lies the West, with all its promise,
But man is like a chained beast,
Left to rot and decay between these walls

My guidance counselor was alerted, and he asked if I were on any special medications. It might have been the parts about the strong arms and fine mind, but I never let piddly lies like that slow me down.

But the roping! Ah, that was where I lived. Now it wasn't really an ideal situation, because when either a horse or a man is learning to rope calves in an arena, it's always good if one or the other of them knows how to do it.

But this didn't stop us!

So what if Tornado thought it was supposed to be a race to see if he could beat the calf down to the end of the arena? So what if, assuming I actually roped one of the darn things as we went by, Tornado wanted to walk up and see what I was doing on the ground with that calf, rather than "working the rope," to help me out?

My Grandma Post, bless her heart, always thought rodeo was cruel. She didn't like the way those cowboys roped the calves and then jerked them around and threw them on the ground and tied their feet together. Then she watched me in a junior rodeo down in Montebello. She was there in the stands with my folks as I backed Tornado into the roping box. I had the tail of my loop tucked under my arm in the time-honored fashion. I had the loop of the piggin' string in my mouth and the tail of it tucked into my belt. I made sure he was set, watching that calf in the chute. I made sure the calf was looking straight ahead. God that was a big calf! Oh well, luck of the draw.

When all was ready, I nodded for the gate and that son of a bitch went flying out of there. A second later, Tornado took off down the arena after him. I waved that loop and threw it

. . . *And I caught him!* Holy Cow! I dragged on the reins and got Tornado actually stopped out there, and I got off him and started down the rope to the calf, and that calf met me halfway.

While I was braced, it didn't do much good, 'cause that sucker jumped up and smacked me in the forehead and then did the Malagueña Spanish Doo-Flop Stomp all over me. My shirt was in tatters, I had to pick up my glasses from the ground twice, and Tornado was standing there watching me do this, rather than backing up and working that rope.

Every time I picked up a hoof to leg the calf down, it bellered and dropped me again and danced a little Irish jig on my head. But finally, because I was more stubborn than the calf, I got him down and hog-tied, and threw both hands in the air, triumphantly.

I looked up at the flag judge, whose arm had been getting tired waiting for me to tie the calf, and I asked him what he thought my time might be.

I believe he said, "Well, it's still Saturday."

I gleefully trotted my bloodied remains over to the stands to bask in my glory, my shirt hanging here and there from my former torso. That was the last time Grandma ever felt sorry for the calves.

During my junior year at Rosemead, I'd had enough. Enough school, enough Los Angeles, enough everything. With my folks' reluctant blessings, I borrowed the car, drove north looking for work, and met Gene Burkhart in Independence. Tornado and I moved to the Owens Valley and discovered we were both better at handling mules and mountains than we were calves. I went to high school in Independence the following year and had fun.

Over the next five years, Tornado and I ran wild horses and wild burros. We led many strings of mules into the high country. We weren't what you'd call *good*, really. But we had fun.

Strangely enough, that horse could run through a lava bed after horses and never miss a step, but could trip and fall on his nose in a graded arena. I was never able to figure that out.

I sold my old pard, Tornado, when I was trying to make ends meet in my attempt at being a first husband.

But he's never far from my heart.

And though some people at the time thought I'd paid too much for him, he gave me my fifty bucks worth, and much more.

THE COYOTE
FAMILY

→

I became acquainted with the coyote family one afternoon while I waited for a suicidal elk with a bow and a bundle of sharp sticks. I was sitting on a slight ridge with my back to a ponderosa pine about 200 yards from the continental divide in southern New Mexico's Gila Mountains.

There's something magical about the Gila. You get down there, you make yourself invisible, and you get real quiet and something is going to happen. You just know it. It's that kind of a hunting ground. What I was hoping for was a huge six-by-six bull, of course, but that isn't the only magical thing that happens in the Gila, and this was one of those afternoons.

I hadn't been there—in full camo and having taken my alfalfa pills for the past four days to acquire invisibility—more than twenty minutes when the family came into view. I caught something moving out of the corner of my eye and here they came, and for the next thirty seconds, they became the jewel I took home from this hunt.

Father came first, walking along fairly slowly. Mother was right behind him. Then the kids. I was close enough that I could see them clearly. The first of the three pups was a female, the two behind her were male.

Sister pup was a serious little coyote. She was trotting along to try to keep up with Mom. But this wasn't easy with two knothead brothers behind her who seemed to think her tail was the most fascinating thing on earth.

First one brother would go up and bite her tail, and she'd turn around, give a warning yip, and try to bite the offending brother. Then she'd get back in line again and try to catch up to Mother. Then the other male pup would come up and give her tail a tug, and she'd try to bite him, too. Finally, Father and Mother Coyote stopped and turned to see what would happen. This pause in the parade gave Sis the opening she was waiting for. She dove headfirst into the most recent offender and bit him good. He yelped and ran behind a bush. Sis looked at the other brother, but he didn't want any part of her.

So Father started off again, followed by Mother and then by Sis, who had a kind of saucy look on her face. The two boys toddled along behind, the one in the rear favoring one hind leg that had been sistered a bit.

In seconds, the whole family had passed within ten yards of me and had gone down the arroyo.

I got to see a little bit of coyote family life, and realized it wasn't all that different from our own. Makes a guy smile.

LITTLE SLIM'S MONUMENTAL BOOGER FEST

I n early June of that beautiful packing year, I was assigned three youngsters to teach the mountains to: two young geldings and a filly.

One of the geldings was a four-year-old named Ranger, the filly was a pretty palomino and I can't remember her name, and the third horse was a little guy, a sorrel blaze-faced gelding who stood about 14.2 hands at the withers and weighed maybe 900 pounds (but only if he had a heavy saddle and a 135-pound cowboy on his back). These were unbroken horses, even Ranger. I guess he'd been out in pasture all his life, and now it was his turn to pack people around and become a tax-paying United States citizen.

I couldn't help having a favorite here, and that was the third one, the little bitty sorrel gelding. He was two years old and I liked his positive attitude about life. He didn't think there was anything too fierce for him to snort at, and he always brought a smile to my face. But I didn't know his name.

"What's the name of that little sorrel?" I asked.

Gene Burkhart, boss man for Sequoia-Kings Pack Trains, thought for a minute, then smiled slightly. "Well, he's kinda goofy, so I think we'll call him Slim."

Starting an unbroken colt is one of the most fun things there is to do. These are kids, youngsters. They aren't bad, just a little snorty, because there's all kinds of strange things going on, and horses are born cowards. So what a trainer has to do is introduce new things to them (known by the scientific term *boogers*) and get them used to them, one at a time. When a horse has had all possible boogers introduced to him, and the snorting has changed to snoring, he's a gentle horse. Now that doesn't mean he's a trained horse, necessarily, but one that is ready to be trained. He can pack you around without jumping off a cliff, and he can be caught, bridled, saddled, and ridden. Hopefully he's learned the word *whoa*. And there you are, in business with a gentle horse. For most riding horses in the world, this is as far as their training ever gets, or is required.

If a guy takes his time, and does it properly, most horses won't buck when first ridden. If you try to rush things, sometimes they get over-boogered and have to find a way out, and this usually involves the collision of back pockets and Mother Earth, and is greatly to be avoided. Pain sometimes follows.

Of course, sometimes you can do everything just right and a horse just has to buck a little bit at first for self-respect, maybe, who knows. That Ranger colt was like that. Sweet horse. Kind eyes. But he lost it a bit and bucked the first time I got on him. It was all over in seconds and he never mentioned it again.

Two weeks after his first saddling, by the way, I rode Ranger into the High Sierra to help another packer. The packer had lost one dude horse up there someplace, so I needed to bring his party out while he hunted for the lost horse. This left the family one horse short, and the horse was for a nine-year-old girl. Strangely enough, she didn't want to be left alone in the mountains without her family, so I put her behind my saddle and we rode Ranger double over an 11,800-foot pass that day. He was that gentle.

Gene about had a fit when I came riding in with a girl behind my saddle on what was officially a green bronc. But

Ranger right then could be ridden safely by anyone, anywhere. He was a good guy.

Most well-bred horses are like Ranger. Calm and steady, reluctant to booger. In a couple of weeks they're pretty well de-snortified and ready for citizenship and fun.

Well, little Slim was a handful. Oh, he didn't buck at all when I first rode him, but he was smart as barbed wire, fascinated by everything around him, and didn't think there was a rock so large or so small that he couldn't blow a little snot on it, just to keep it in line and properly aware of what a marvelous beast he was.

I rode Slim down at the ranch for a couple of weeks, and then I put shoes on him and we took him "up the hill" to the pack station at Onion Valley, a meadow at 9,200 feet some fourteen miles west of Independence.

I threw him into the horse corral and waited for the right time to take him into the mountains. I didn't want to go over the pass with him yet, as there were a lot of rock piles and steep stuff up there. I was waiting for something easy, close, and quick for his maiden voyage.

Before a week had gone by, we got it. A trail crew from the Inyo National Forest needed to be packed in to Gilbert Lake, a mere three miles from the pack station, and on the same side of the pass. Gilbert! Perfect. Oh yes, this was a piece of cake. I rubbed Slim's ears and nose and told him what a good little boy he was going to be the next day on his first trip.

He looked at me with those big kind eyes and blew some handy snot on my neck.

The morning of the trip, I had (I think) three trail crew guys, all their gear, and then their trail-improvement stuff. It was the latter that was interesting. We had two mule loads of dynamite (naturally, the blasting caps went on a third mule), we had shovels and axes and all that stuff, and, most fascinating of all, an eight-foot-long pry bar. Picture a crowbar with the hook straightened out, eight feet long, weighing probably seventy-five or eighty pounds, with a flat beveled edge on one end and a point on the other. This called for the skills of Coalie, a black mule who was a solid veteran and was also a lumber mule. A lumber mule is a treasure. He is trained to carry the tail end of a bunch of boards on his pack saddle, on the top of which is a big swivel deal. Picture a lazy Susan on top of a saddle. Then the mule in front and the lumber mule behind have these boards tied to them like an eight-legged hook-and-ladder truck. Coalie knew to duck his head under the pry bar, and go wide on the switchbacks. He carried the trickiest load, so I led him and strung the other pack mules behind him.

At this point, Coalie had about two feet of pointed pry bar sticking out in front of his head and he looked a lot like a very dark unicorn heading up the mountain.

I got the forest guys mounted. They were all experienced, so I didn't have to worry about them. Then I took the string of five mules, with Coalie right behind my colt's butt, and started up the trail.

Oh, little Slim horse was doing beautifully. I was so proud of him. Of course, he did have the boogers and snorts, but that was only to be expected. After all, what would you do if you were a young horse working faithfully on your first trip, and walking along with your nose about six inches off the ground to personally inspect each foothold on the trail, and then you discover that someone has sneaked up ahead of you, and right next to the trail has planted a SIXTY-FOOT PINE TREE! Hey, don't tell me you wouldn't snort, too.

So we continued without any real problems up the mountain, having thoroughly snot-soaked the trees, boulders, and one lady trying to have a quiet picnic. I was so proud of that little guy. He was walking carefully, each step, and we weren't setting any land speed records, but we didn't care. We were only going three miles, and if it took us all morning that would just mean the trail crew wouldn't have to start using those shovels and axes quite as quickly, and they all seemed to think they could wait with no problem at all.

Well, just before you get to Gilbert Lake—I mean 100 yards before you get to Gilbert Lake—there is a big rockslide, where huge boulders mingle with not-so-huge boulders, and the trail goes across this for maybe 50 yards, and then you pitch camp at Gilbert Lake and catch a fish or something.

Slim reached this rockslide and it flummoxed him for a minute, but only for a minute. He got his head back down there in ground-checking position again and started across. In this position it's hard to see what's ahead of you, but Slim wasn't in tourist mode yet, but still struggling along in sure-footed mode. It's better to be safe than sorry.

That's why he didn't see what I saw ahead of us. Up ahead there about eight feet was a boulder the size of a small car standing on end and just above it was a little yellow flag waving slowly back and forth. At this point I was a fairly seasoned eastern High Sierra packer, and knew the names of a lot of the varmints in the woods, but this one threw me at first. Then the light bulb came on. Of course! It was a Los Angeles back-packer, hiding behind this giant rock, and he had a backpack on, and the backpack had a fishing rod tied to it, and there was a yellow flag flying at the tip of the rod. I looked at this, and looked down at my young chum walking so conscientiously beneath me, unaware of the impending catastrophe, and I only had time to say something under my breath that started with "Please, Lord, no . . . !!!"

And then the backpacker (who wore a blaze orange cap and looked like a Martian escapee) whipped around three feet in front of Slim's nose, waved his hand and said, "Hi!"

As Slim's eyes bugged out, they noticed the wildly wagging yellow flag on the end of the fishing rod, and the stupid look on the Martian's face (by this time, little Slim had him pegged as a Martian horse eater) and the little fellow remembered reading nothing whatever in the text "How to Be a Gentle American Riding Horse" about having to face boogers like this one. This was a home-run booger. This was a record-book booger. This booger flew completely past the scary line and soared into the realm of bad dreams and cannibalistic pretense.

Slim then threw it full-bore into reverse.

Remember what was right behind us? Coalie? Cast iron unicorn? Coalie had his head down, too, and didn't see the colt jumping backwards at him until little Slim had pretty thoroughly goosed himself on that pry bar. With a beller that could be heard in San Francisco, Slim jumped headlong up the hill into the rock pile, hopping from granite to granite, telling the world that he'd changed his mind and this wasn't as much fun as he'd thought it would be. In the meantime, I was trying to turn my string of mules loose, because they, too, were forced to follow us up into that rocky mess. By the time I was able to take the dallies off that saddle horn and concentrate on calming Slim down, I had three pack mules full of explosives up in those rocks. The blast, I knew, would be heard for a great distance. The only thing that made my impending demise tolerable was I knew at least I'd take that miserable Martian backpacking peckerwood sonofabitch with me.

Finally, little Slim stopped up on a big rock, looked down at the backpacker, and saluted him with a snot shower.

The backpacker, not realizing what had just happened, looked up at one of the trail crew guys and said, "What's wrong with that guy's horse?"

The veteran mountain rider looked down from his horse and said, "Son, if you are real smart, you won't ask him about that."

In less than half an hour, I'd managed to get little Slim down on the trail again and get everybody safely camped, dynamite and all, at Gilbert Lake.

And Slim? He made a wonderful horse for those mountains. I was really proud of him. Some of the later packers in his life wondered why it always took him so long to cross that rock slide this side of Gilbert Lake, but I didn't say anything. Buddies don't rat each other out.

THE
BUCKSKIN STUD
FICTION

▶

The tracks of a large bunch of unshod horses were beneath our own shod hooves then, and Chuckles raised his head higher, ears still working. We started up an arroyo and then Chuckles stopped, quivering, his head up and his ears slammed forward into a point.

I slipped down and took several deep knee bends to loosen up, then buckled hobbles on Chuckles and tied the reins to the connecting strap. I took off the chaps, put a sneak on the lip of the next rise, and peeked over.

There they were.

Hundreds of wild horses in the sage-dotted valley were before me, mostly bays and blacks with some buckskins sprinkled through the herd like salt. I lay still and watched them move, these horses that had never felt a rope. They grazed, and then looked up and around, so the herd looked like a symphony of bobbing heads.

The herd was actually a number of herds, each subgroup with its own stallion and lead mare. The lead mare always picked out the deepest, choicest grass, kicking any who challenged her. The stallion circled his portion of the mares and babies, looking threateningly at anyone who came close.

This was repeated time and again across this valley between hills of swelling yellow dirt and black killer rocks. Always the same. A little dance of vigilance, if you will. Freedom has its price. And there was a symmetry, a balance to it.

The nearest horses were maybe two hundred yards in front of me and the wind was right in my face, so this was the best approach. From the time we topped the ridge, it would be only seconds before the horses were in flight. I looked down the hill at Chuckles and saw him at full alert, but quiet and still. A nervous pawing this far away would be enough to send a stallion to investigate, or maybe they would just all panic and quit the country. When it comes to a good first-cabin panic, horses wrote the book. The hobbles were a good idea.

At this distance, there may be some horsemen who can pick out a good horse, a sound horse, or a young horse. That is what I wanted, of course. But there's no way I could pick one out at two hundred yards. Oh, maybe if one were missing a leg, I could see him limp from that far away and scratch him off the list, but that would be about it. So I lay there, in no hurry to break this pastoral scene into its component parts of violent hooves and snaking rope.

I realize there are big herds of wild horses running loose all over the West right now, but it's hard to ignore reality. The handwriting is on the wall for wild horses. Yes, they are protected now, but only from people who would catch and use them. They are prey to crowding, disease, starvation, and death. They are protected from the mustangers now, but that will have to change. I'm afraid I have no faith in the common sense of any governmental group. It's as though there is an equation saying the more minds put to solving a problem, the less common sense the answer will have. If Congress made a mistake by not allowing anyone at all to catch wild horses, it will more than likely try to rectify that by wiping them all out. But even if lightning were to strike the funny building with the round roof, and a compromise was found, the horses are likely to come out short, anyway. Horses like land and grass and water. So do people.

That might be of some use as an epitaph for these animals someday.

So I lay there and just watched them. Lay there until I could feel every pebble beneath me, digging into my skin. Lay there until my arms went to sleep. And as I watched them, I thought of the refrain hunters of the north secretly said to themselves high on a tundra ridge just before making a final stalk on the ocean of palmated antlers that was a migrating herd of caribou: "I wonder which of you grazing peacefully right now will have his life change drastically in the next few minutes. Your life will change and so will mine, but only I can decide that."

I looked back down the hill at my horse, quivering his sleek muscles beneath his new, slick summer coat. He was in shape. I was in shape. We came here to do a job, and by smash, let's go rope a wild horse.

It took only a small tightening to bring the cinches up snug. I buckled on the chaps and checked the horn knot on the catch rope. Snug and tight. A glance showed all four shoes were on and ready.

This was it. Checked everything. When we topped that rise, I wanted to be in overdrive. I stepped aboard, built a loop in the nylon catch rope, and ran my hand along the back of Chuckles's neck just to be friendly. Then I touched him with those rowels and we hopped over the ridge and shot down into the tailings of that panicked herd like demons.

Necks were bobbing, like fish spawning upstream, but there was a sea of necks, with forelocks and manes flying, and tails, and some broke off to the left and to the right, and we let them go. The old stuff and the very young broke off and went around, but the necks ahead of us now, fifty yards ahead of us, were in for the fight. They were in for the chase, and so were we.

Chuckles scattered gravel so smoothly that I just kept the tail of the loop tucked beneath my armpit and watched around me at the multicolored sea through which we sailed so effortlessly.

Then there were two ahead, flying, seeming to fly, floating along through the sage like pounding ghosts. A sorrel and a buckskin. Both clean-limbed and floating, flying in this old, old dance. And it was our turn to dance it with them. Thank you. The buckskin took my fancy, so when the two separated, I nudged Chuckles's head toward the buckskin, and the sorrel flaked off and back like a jet fighter peeling out of formation.

And then it was us and the buckskin. I yelled, "Hello!" at this horse, then gave an "Eeeeeeeha!" and leaned forward as if I could help Chuckles along. And the buckskin we chased in this old sweet dance was a banshee devil of the mountains, diving into arroyos, charging into lava beds, and then opening new bursts of speed out on the flats. But at last it was a long flat before us, reaching off to the south, this one, and we'd have a long run and a good run, and this was what we'd waited for, because the yards between us diminished as though in slow motion. Forty, then thirty, then twenty.

The weeks of grain for Chuckles and the running and conditioning were paying off. The inborn speed he got from his father had evened things up between a riderless wild animal and this two-part unit of ours that was trying to work.

And then the bobbing neck was there, and I felt Chuckles throw an extra spurt into it. He knew his business and this was it. And then the loop was up and was swinging and I threw.

The loop flopped alongside the horse's neck and quickly slid off. I built another loop as Chuckles continued to rate this wild horse ahead of us. And the loop was now ready and came up for a swing, and somehow I knew this time. Then through the morning music of the mountains and the violence of our little dance here in front of God, I could hear the words of Ross, so many years ago, when I missed a calf.

"You soft-looped him," he'd said. "You throw that rope like an old lady, you'll never catch anything."

So I did as I was told and concentrated on that spot just behind the ears where the little bump lived, and I swung that rope and Chuckles laid his ears back a bit tighter, and then I stared a burning tunnel through that little bump by the horse's ears and threw that loop the way I'd pitch a baseball at that one little spot.

The loop whipped out, the honda touching that bump. Then the loop flared out around, dropped over the horse's head, and I grabbed the rope and pulled the slack taut.

Chuckles sat down hard in the sagebrush, but this wasn't some calf to be flipped, but a 900-pound horse, so I just had time to say oh-dear-Jesus when all hell hit the end of that rope and all three of us went down.

Looking back on it now, I still don't know how that horse managed to stay beneath me. Before I had time to bail out, some sagebrush whipped my face and then we were up again, and I was still in the saddle, and we were back in business and securely tied to a screaming wild animal trying to fling his various parts to the four corners of the earth. For the first time, as we dodged and danced and faced this dervish, I saw we'd roped ourselves a young stud horse.

He screamed and plunged, then fell and got up and plunged and screamed, then made one run for us, but changed his mind before he got there and shot off to the left and damn near jerked us down again when he came to the end of that thirty feet of nylon catch rope.

And there was old Chuckles, just working rope like we were in an arena with the stopwatch on us. We were both sweating, and the little mustang was sweating, and it was a bit like tying onto a large grayling with a two-pound tippet on the fly rod. We'd give a little, then back up and take a little, and that buckskin was giving it holy bananas with all four feet. No quit in this rascal, I thought. He'd be a good horse. He'd do, for sure.

But he finally just lay back against that rope, made chok-ing sounds, and toppled over. I untied one length of rope I had behind the cantle and stepped off Chuckles to go down and claim our horse. Chuckles kept the rope just taut, and I ran down and tied a large bowline around the horse's neck, then flipped a loop of rope around one hind pastern and drew it up toward the loop and tied it off. He wouldn't be moving too fast in that foot rope.

I grabbed the loop around the horse's neck and gave a quick jerk to loosen it enough to let some more air in, and that buckskin sucker jumped up and reached for me with those teeth while I was making it back to the saddle in record time.

Well, the foot rope and my smell so close to his nostrils gave the little guy another dose of the fighting fantods, and he went to it again. The foot rope made him panic some more, and he did his grunts and flips and strikes the best he could. Then he went down again.

This time I slipped off my Levi jacket and pulled it over his face, tying the sleeves under his throatlatch to blindfold him. He lay stretched out and quivering. The fight was done. When that blind comes down and the lights go out, the tough-est horse in the world shuts 'er down.

I took down some more rope and fixed a rope halter on him, then ran the catch rope through it and through the neck rope and fixed it fast around his girth. When this was done, I snapped the catch rope at Chuckles and backed him into the slack, then eased my jacket off the mustang's face and trotted back to the saddle. But this time he lay there and breathed hard and looked at us.

So I talked to him, and Chuckles did, too, in a way. We just sat there, this unlikely trio in the middle of a desert mountain range, and we told him things weren't that bad. And while I spoke, I looked down at this sleek wild animal with my ropes all over him. He looked kind of pitiful, trussed up that way, but if you looked in his eyes and tried to think like he did, he looked kind of cute, too. I began to like him.

When his breathing became regular again, he lurched to his feet, making it on the third try. He looked at everything and sniffed everything and twitched around a lot, but mostly he just looked at us standing there talking to him.

It was still morning, and there was no panic for time, so I thought we'd just try and talk him gentle. I believe it worked, too.

I just explained to him that being wild wasn't such a good idea for a horse, because there weren't any guarantees on feed that way. And being a stud horse out there in the Cosos? Hey, you could find better deals than that. If you weren't the biggest and toughest and rankest stud horse on the mountain, you were going to be off living a pretty lonely life with some other bachelors. And let's say you were the rankest old bronc in the country. What that brought you was a life of scars and bruises and tooth marks just from trying to hold onto what was yours. It was not fun, mustang, remember that. Wouldn't it be nice to just take a day or two off in some green pasture and play around with your pals? Fun stuff. Horse stuff. Why, there'd be some flesh on your young tough bones, my friend.

And he listened, I think. He stood there watching us, his head stretched out toward us as he drank in the wind from our sweaty bodies. And he swirled the new smells around in his big black nostrils and tasted every nuance of scent, setting it in his mind. He shook his head, then stretched out for more scent. Twice he fell back against the rope, but that was all, because with the elaborate rig I had on him, sometimes called a "cowboy's come-along," when he hit the end of that rope, it squeezed him around the girth and shot him forward, and with the rope run through his makeshift halter, he was forced to face us.

For more than an hour old Chuckles and I had a visit with this wild horse. He was still plenty alert, but that look of panic wasn't there any more.

Years back a wonderful professional roper told me the only thing dumber than a horse was an earthworm, but not everyone agreed with him. One cowboy who was there said that was unkind to earthworms, and put the intelligence quotient of a horse flapping senselessly somewhere between that of today's domesticated turkey and a flat brown rock.

Because a horse is not, in fact, an intellectual prairie fire, it takes a little longer for some things to sink in. Like capture. We sat there talking to this buckskin for a long time and finally you could see the acceptance in his eyes. Yes, mustangs are wild, but only until you show them they aren't anymore. I've always believed in keeping total control of the situation, then going one step at a time, and giving the old pony time to get used to each step. My theory is that horses would learn more quickly if the trainers would just go off and read a book for an hour each time they introduced something new.

Finally I stepped down and started down the rope to the mustang. This took maybe ten minutes, talking softly all the time. To a horse, ten minutes is a short time. By the time I reached for his neck and touched him, he was ready enough for me that he just stood there and quivered but took it. After all, he was still alive, and I hadn't done any of the things necessary to kill him or eat him, which is what he expected from this situation. I rubbed his neck and withers and talked to him a lot more, and while he didn't like it, he decided to tolerate it. It takes time for those messages to sink in through layers of bone and gristle, but once they register, it seems to be all right.

I talked to this horse and petted him until he was quiet and as content as a horse is able to be when he's lashed up like Joan of Arc at a barbecue. Then I went way around him and approached him from the other side. Naturally, he acted as though he'd never seen me before, so we had to start all over again getting acquainted on the other side. Horses are like that. We got to the neck petting part and talking until both sides of this bronc were petting proof.

He began to relax, and I slipped my jacket over his head again. He made one jump, but then lay back against the rope and stopped while I tied the sleeves to blindfold him. Then I took off the foot rope, letting his hind leg down to the ground, walked back to Chuckles, and tied that foot rope behind the cantle where I'd gotten it. I rode Chuckles slowly up to the wild horse, who quivered and blew as he smelled Chuckles approaching but was frozen in his tracks by the blindfold.

We talked to him another ten minutes, maybe, then I reached down and pulled off the jacket.

And he stood there, two feet away, just looking at us.

I reached over and touched him on the neck, and rubbed that a little, telling him it was going to be all right, then I turned Chuckles toward the catch pen down in the canyon and rode away. When the rope tightened, the mustang fought it, then came up a little. Then we started off and he fought it again, and we waited until he was through and had time to cool off, then we started again.

He began taking a step or two toward us, then we'd ride a step or two ahead and take the slack out of the rope. He'd walk forward, and we'd walk forward. In another thirty minutes, he'd figured out how this was supposed to work and figured out we weren't there to hurt him. He followed us down the canyon and across the flat, and two hours later I led him into the catch pen and closed the gate.

THE SEARCH
FOR THE
SECRET LAKE

→

I know it's there, that secret lake of mine. In all the years I lived in the cabin down the mountain from it with Pam, I was never able to find it, but that doesn't mean it isn't there.

It's on the maps, you see. You look on the topo map of that piece of Alaska, and there's this dark little lake-shaped blob right where the forest meets the tundra. Right there in what we guides know as the "hunting zone." Where the transition is from tundra down to forest, there is a belt of alders, and it's in these alder hells (yes, that's what they're called, with good reason) where the grizzlies and the big bull moose live. It's the area where the wolves come down to hunt, even in the summer. It's the one area where you see wolverine before the snows of winter blanket the land.

And right there, just before the tundra stretches up toward the high center and caribou country of the Talkeetna Mountains, is a little alcove in the mountains. A little tuck in the golf-course-like country of the big bear. And in that cove is my lake.

"You don't know if there's a lake there," said a close friend with many more years than I had in the Bush. "Those maps were all made from aerial photos. Probably no one has ever been there. No one has ever surveyed that country, anyway. That's for sure. That could just be a shadow falling across that little canyon there and they think it could be a lake."

I nodded, as though in wisdom, but I know it's there.

We hadn't lived there a full year before I took the rifle and a couple of huskies and hiked up there. You have to realize this is thick birch forest, with a generous sprinkling of spruce. There are areas where you can't see more than twenty yards ahead or to the sides. I climbed through those thick trees and waist-deep high-bush cranberries and fiddlehead ferns until I hit the tundra, and I ranged along, looking down, hoping to see my lake. If I found it, I probably wouldn't build a cabin on it or anything. I just wanted to go there. I just wanted to see it. I just wanted to silently and privately plant the nonexistent Flag of Slim on it and claim it as a heart-place of my own.

But I didn't find it.

Pam said I should use a compass the next time, but there's a heavy declination that far north (the magnetic pole is northeast of there), and figuring out declinations and coefficients and coaxials and codependents just makes my brain hurt.

It was about two years later when I made the next attempt. The canyon that empties out into our tiny Trinity Creeks Valley (we found it, so we got to name it) didn't pan out for me the first time, so I went up to Joe's Lake, a mile away, and went up the ridge behind that lake.

Again, I finally wove my way through the alder thickets and then into the open tundra country (saw a huge bull moose this time) but still no lake.

In the years we lived there, I must have worn out that map trying to figure a way up there. It's less than five miles from the cabin, if it is a lake.

Oh, it's a lake. It may only be a lake in my mind, but it's a lake. I'll tell you all about it, too. I know it's a beautiful little lake. There are some trees down at the lower end, not really tall ones, being up that high of course. And the tundra rises from the east side of the lake. You can get a great view of Mt. McKinley from that little lake. When the wind is still you can see the huge massif of the mountain reflected in the ice cold waters. I mean, you can just look on the map and see it.

Lots of animals come there to drink, and there are both trout and grayling for the catching in that little lake of mine. Like most of the lakes in Alaska, it doesn't have a name.

Maybe it's a dream lake. But it's my dream lake, anyway. It goes down on my life list of places I want to visit some-day. Cartagena, Colombia. Cougar, Washington. Presque Isle, Maine. And the lonely little lake somewhere up there, just out of sight, just where the tundra takes over from the trees.

A private little part of Alaska. A private little part of the world. My lake.

I *know* it's up there. And someday . . .

Oh yes.

Leona the
Hotcake Mule

————————————————————————————————➤

I t was all about seven spots below the stripe. That's what
they told me, those fish biologists. That's why we were
here at this remote camp in the eastern High Sierra. That's
why I would be packing five-gallon cans full of water and fish
eggs and milt on down the mountain to where the trucks are
waiting. Seven spots below the stripe. "On these golden trout,"
one of them told me, "we can tell they're pure goldens if they
don't have more than seven spots below the stripe."

So I took the biologists in to Cottonwood Lakes, which
is the ancestral home of the golden trout. Cottonwood Lakes
and a stretch nearby of the headwaters of the Kern River are
where goldens were found. Everywhere else they've been
planted by humans.

These biologists had, in those days, a one-room shack con-
sisting of plywood with a corrugated tin roof. It had one door
and a window. This was the bunkhouse, kitchen, and everything else for these guys. That's why I tried to warn them when
they started fixing pancakes.

They did it inside this cabin, you see.

The stock was quietly grazing around the other side of this
lake, but I knew that wouldn't last too long, as I watched the

designated breakfast biologist spoon that batter onto the skillet on the Coleman stove.

"How much batter do you have?" I asked.

"Oh, we have lots, Slim. Don't worry. There's plenty for you."

"I'm not the one you have to worry about," I told him. "Leona will be over here pretty soon."

"Leona?"

"That pretty little appaloosa mule," I said. "She has a . . . well, a *thing* about hotcakes."

He laughed. "Well, she'll have to wait her turn," he said.

Of course, he forgot to check with Leona on that waiting-a-turn part, and she never was real big on waiting. Where she decided to wait was right in the doorway, half in and half out of the cabin. This created a problem because the pancakes were in the cabin and the rest of the biologists were out of the cabin. A pancake would have to get past Leona's teeth to reach the crew.

That wasn't going to happen.

She went through two big bowls of batter before she walked away and let the biologists get their breakfast.

GILBERT THE
MEXICAN JINX

→

"It's no use, Slim," he said, dejectedly from the sleeping bag for about the fourth time that morning, "Let's face it, I'm just a Mexican jinx." Then Gilbert Villanueva whipped out a handkerchief and blew his nose in such a nuclear-devicive fashion that the wall tent expanded and contracted with the force.

Gilbert was on one of our late hunts, which, loosely translated into guide talk, means cold hunts. There were a few inches of snow already on the ground, clinging to Alaska with hopes of spending the entire winter. The temperature was 20 below at times.

Now why Gilbert considered himself to be a jinx is anyone's guess, because he'd already taken a beautiful caribou bull with me. That happened out of main camp, and it caused quite a bit of concern. Gilbert Villanueva was a Hispanic truck driver from the Los Angeles suburb (and not a really fancy one) of Pico Rivera. In fact, Gilbert drove for a freight line, and didn't even own the truck. He lived with his family in a modest subdivision, and he drove a truck between Los Angeles and Tucson.

This is not the typical profile of one of our hunters. Most of our hunters fell into the financial category of industrialists and movie stars. An Alaska guided hunt can be a lot of things, but cheap isn't one of them. I had to ask Gilbert about this, as we got to know each other, because this was not common.

"Well, Slim," he said, "I don't drink, I don't go bowling, I don't drive hot rods. I hunt. I save my money and I go hunting. I've been to Africa, too, you know."

We were in one of Clark Engle's camps on the west side of the Alaska Range. Gilbert was in his early fifties, I'd guess, and just days before the hunt began he'd had some surgery, I forget what kind, that slowed him down in the woods some. But he wasn't going to pass up the chance to go for an Alaska hunt just because he was sore. So here he came.

The caribou was a beautiful bull that Gilbert shot way up on a huge tundra ridge about three miles from main camp that Clark called John Bailey Ridge, after one of his favorite hunters. John Bailey Ridge, in the spring and the fall, was a freeway for caribou. They'd come sometimes in dribbles, sometimes in herds of several thousand. In large numbers, it was fairly easy to find them, as the steam from their breath and urine would create a moving cloud above them as they walked along. In case you've ever wondered about the Eskimo game of blanket toss, where a person is trampolined as high into the air as he can go, it dates back to the simple hunt for caribou. In areas like northwestern Alaska, where it is totally flat and without trees, the blanket toss elevates a person just enough to spot that cloud of caribou breath.

On the day Gilbert got his caribou, we saw the steam rising from the ridge and saw, through the spotting scope, that it resembled an ant hill, covered top to bottom and end to end with caribou. This was the big fall migration for the herd. Gilbert and I went as quickly as his stitches would allow us, as we tried to get ahead of the herd.

That didn't work. The main part of the herd had already passed by the time we got up on the ridge. There was a lot of stopping and resting, and I was young and eager at that time, and not as patient as I should have been with Gilbert. He was doing the best he could under the circumstances, though, so by the time we got up on the ridge and were hidden in one of those tundra "foxholes" that occur here and there, probably three or four thousand caribou had passed that spot already.

But there were more.

We hid in the foxhole and waited. Caribou came and split and went around the foxhole, but it was all cows and calves. Occasionally we would see a nice set of those delicate-looking antlers above the backs of the animals, but those herd bulls had surrounded themselves with cows for protection— protection from wolves and protection from us, too, as it turned out. Any bullet would have to pass through a half-dozen caribou before reaching one of those herd bulls, so we just sat quietly and waited.

Gilbert kept apologizing for having been so slow, and I kept telling him it was no big deal. I told him any minute now that bull of his would be along. I told it better than I believed it, of course, but I knew it was either going to happen or it wasn't. That's why they call it hunting instead of shooting.

Then the caribou kinda dribbled away to just about nothing. Some older cows straggling along behind the others. An occasional calf without a mother.

Then up along the ridge came a small group of bulls. These were what we called "bachelor bulls." They didn't have any cows because they were either young bulls who weren't old enough to fight well yet, old bulls who couldn't fight well any longer, or regular bulls who just couldn't fight well enough to get any cows. They had been whipped out of the main herds by the herdmasters, and they traveled together at the tag end of the big herds, probably for companionship as well as for safety.

Quietly we glassed them as they came. Some were too small, some were big but had broken tines from fighting. Then there he was at the end of the group. Magnificent. He was a very old bull, and the width of his antlers was declining each year, but the points! He was beautiful. A mass of points, a double shovel guarding his face, and huge bez points. I pointed him out to Gilbert, and he nodded quietly and got ready, and then the bull was his and we were alone with his bull on that grand old ridge.

By the time I'd unzipped and caped and subdivided that caribou, it was getting dark. Dark, and very cold. The combination of surgery, exercise, and a long day left Gilbert barely able to move, let alone make it back to camp, so I decided we would "siwash it" out there in the woods for the night.

I got the caribou parts moved down into some timber not far away and got a fire built near a couple of very large rocks. We heard Clark's Super Cub in the air as he flew in circles in the waning light, and I knew he was looking for us and was worried we weren't back in camp. He didn't fly out far enough to see our fire or he wouldn't have been so concerned.

So Gil and I spent some partly uncomfortable, partly very special hours together, eating caribou ribs, telling lies and jokes, reminiscing about earlier days in southern California (I grew up about five miles from Pico Rivera, in El Monte). We also had quite a time thinking up just how much we'd be willing to pay for a cup of coffee.

We dozed and fed the fire, and laughed at each other, and it was just fine. In the morning we had more of the ribs and started back for camp. This time, Clark saw us walking, circled once, wagged his wings, and then flew straight toward camp. He did this in case we'd gotten turned around and needed to know where camp was.

It might have been that special night of the caribou that caused Gil to catch cold. Who knows? But the fact is, he did catch cold. His sneezing was monumental, his nose blowing was atomic, and his cough caused the spruce trees to shake in terror.

But he still wanted a moose, so we went out to a camp that was very productive for late-season moose. There was another hunter and another guide there. They already had a moose and were looking for caribou. So for several days, Gil and I hunted one direction out of camp and the other two hunted out the other way. Then in the evening, they'd tell us of the big bull moose they'd seen that day, and we hadn't seen any. So the next day, we'd go where they'd gone the previous day and wouldn't see anything, and they'd go where we'd gone, and that evening tell us about the huge bull they'd seen that day.

This nightmare went on for several days, and so did Gil's cold. He was just feeling miserable, and it was very cold, and he finally just said he thought he'd stay in camp and keep warm rather than go hunting. But I wouldn't let him. I teased and bullied him each morning until he'd finally give in and get dressed and we'd go out and not see anything but clouds and tracks. Clark's camps were fair chase all the way. I'd like to explain this. I was teasing and bullying him because I love to hunt and didn't want to stay in camp, and because I really wanted him to get a moose. If he didn't get a moose, it didn't cost Clark any money. Clark charged so much per day to hunt. Period. If you got five animals, same price. If you got no animals, same price. If you wanted to stay in camp and read a book, go ahead. No skin off our butts. Some camps charged a basic price for camp, and then tacked on trophy fees of thousands of dollars if the hunter was successful. I think in those days, the going trophy fee in some of those camps for a black bear was about $800, with $1,200 for a moose, and maybe $2,500 for sheep or grizzly. So those guides were under pressure to produce dead animals for their bosses. They also didn't have the luxury we did of honestly telling your hunter "Let's wait. I think we can find you a better bear than that one."

On this last day of his ten-day hunt, Gil really didn't want to go, but I terrorized him enough to agree to walk only a couple of hundred yards to where we could sit down and look for moose.

I led the way into the slamming cold morning. Gilbert followed along at a shuffle behind me. Every so often he'd pull out his handkerchief and blow his nose. It could be heard a long way. I'd shush him and he'd just shrug and say, "Why bother, Slim? We aren't going to see anything, anyway. I tell you, I'm a Mexican jinx, that's all."

We'd made about 200 yards from the tent when the ol' nose had to blow again. The hollow, ringing sheer decibels of the blown nose made me jump in that hushed quiet that is winter in Alaska. I spun around, raising my finger toward my lips to shush Gil again when I heard this very loud grunt.

"Unnnnh—UNNNNNNH"

Bull moose. We both froze. I needed to hear that bull again to pinpoint his location. I grunted.

Nothing.

I whispered to Gil, "Blow your nose again."

He whipped out that hankie and honked a world-class nose blow.

Right away the answer came.

"Unnnnh- UNNNNNNNNH!"

I had the bull locked in on nose-blower radar now. We silently started in that direction. After a hundred yards, I still didn't see him, so I motioned for Gil to give it another honk. He did. And got an answer, too.

"UNNNNNNH!"

Just over the rise . . . right there. I told Gil to put one in the chamber and put the safety on and walk next to me. We sneaked up to the top of this little rise and . . . looking straight at us from maybe twenty-five yards away were three huge bulls. They froze. We froze.

"The one on the left," I whispered.

Bang.

At that moment, our relationship changed. We had been hunter and guide, of course, and we were really getting to be friends, too. But when that bull fell that day out near the Swift Fork of the Kuskokwim River, we became a very special brand of hunting buddies. Here's how it worked.

For several years after that, and until Gil died, I'd get the occasional telephone call. The caller usually sounded as if he'd gone partly through a six pack, too.

"Is this Slim?"

"Yes it is."

"Well, Slim, my name is Daniel (or Pedro, or David), and I'm a friend of Gilbert Villanueva's."

"Yes, it's true, Daniel. I was there. Gilbert called in that bull moose by blowing his nose."

"Oh damn! I lost ten bucks!"

Glad to do it, Gil. Anytime at all, amigo.

RAVEN'S
CHILDREN

————————————➤

I n the spring of 1970, I flew into the tiny Tlingit Indian village of Angoon, on Admiralty Island in southeast Alaska. My job with *The Anchorage Daily News* often sent me to strange and wonderful places, and Angoon was one of the best. The Tlingit people have a long and rich heritage which shows up in their art work, their carved totem poles, and their songs and dances. And in their stories.

In the village of Angoon in those days, in a house on the edge of the forest, lived a very old woman named Maggie John. She was from the village of Yakutat, another Tlingit village, but lived in Angoon with her grandchildren and great-grandchildren. Her job, she often told me, was to tell the children what happened to their ancestors, which she called simply The People.

And so, one day when the rains came and the children huddled by the fire in the moss-covered wooden house, Grandma Maggie John told them the story of when the Athabascan warriors from the North forced the Tlingit People to move to the sea during the last Ice Age.

These days, every time it rains, I can still hear her beautiful voice.

You awoke this morning, children, to the sound of the sea. You filled your senses with salt air and with the fragrance of fog bringing you the secrets of the spruce.

You heard the cry of the sea birds and felt beneath your young feet the slickness of the beach rocks and the padded carpet of your beloved forest.

And you think it was always so, my children. You think you have always been children of the sea. You think the raven and the eagle have always watched your comings and goings. That your fathers and grandfathers have always been men of the water.

But hear me, children of the fog, it was not always so.

Once, long before time, long before memory, the People hunted moose instead of deer.

There was once a time when the People lived on the other side of the Snow Mountains. A time when the People, your people, lived where the trees are small and the winter winds blow dry and cold.

Where the People lived, the rivers ran big and swift and the brown bears are smaller than here by the sea.

The People lived there and hunted there. Their boats were small then, and fast. And when winter came, the dogs pulled their sleds quickly across the frozen land.

For timeless seasons, for lives and lives and hundreds of lives come and gone, the People lived across the mountains in the land of the small trees.

It was hard, those times. When the wolves ate the moose, there was hunger. When the caribou did not come, there was hunger. And there was death.

When the dry snows came, and the cloud blanket pulled back, there was Cold come to the People. Cold. A cold like you children have never known.

It was a cold that drives you close to the fire. It was a cold that made the old men spend the long darkness of night heating rocks in the fires, so the rocks could be taken into the lodges to keep death from the children.

It was a cold that stung the skin and turned the rivers to stone and made the caribou leave the land of the People.

And there was hunger and death. Always hunger and death.

And Raven saw his children die and he wept.

Then came to the People a great cold. A cold beyond any that the oldest grandmothers had known. And the snows grew deep, and the canyons became white with snow, and the ice didn't leave the waters.

The People were afraid. The People died. Many old ones died. Many children died. And the moose walked away toward the noon sun.

And with the cold and deep snow came the Enemy. He came from the land of the North Wind. He came to where the People lived, and he wanted the land for himself, because his own land was now just snow. His own land was hills of snow, mountains of snow, and there was nothing left to eat.

And so a war began.

The Enemy were numbered beyond the salmon in the summer rivers and the trees on the land. The People were killed, and their homes taken. Some of the People became slaves for the Enemy. There was hunger and death and the people were pushed back to the Snow Mountains. They were pushed back to the high country where there is no shelter, no wood for fires. There is nothing to eat but the white sheep of the high rocks.

And there was suffering.

The People banded together and walked toward the noon sun, always toward the noon sun. Day after day they walked, carrying the children. And at night, death came to the old and the weak.

But then the People came to the river of the Stikine and saw that its waters flowed fast into the mystery of the Snow Mountains.

And there the People talked. They talked of taking the river to a new land where there would be no enemy. They talked of finding a land where there would be food and the cold would stay far away.

But they saw only the swiftness of the waters of the Stikine and saw there only the swiftness of certain death.

And always behind them came the Enemy, first taking the moose, and then even the white sheep of the Snow Mountains.

So the People built a boat to go down the river. But who could they send? Children were too small to take care of themselves. The young women were needed to cook the food and care for the children. The men were needed for hunting and war and to carry the heavy loads. They talked about this for a long time. Finally they put into this boat the two oldest grandmothers of the People. And they pushed the boat into the water of the Stikine and watched it be pulled into the mystery of the canyon below. And the children wept, as they knew they would never see their beloved grandmothers again.

And the People had placed, high on the Snow Mountains, young men with the eyesight of the eagle and the white sheep. And these men watched down the long mountain drop toward the setting sun. They looked down into a world of fog and clouds and mystery, and saw nothing as the day went on.

And then, just before the night came, the clouds pulled away and they saw the sea shining like silver, far below. And on the sea they saw the little boat and the two grandmothers on it and the grandmothers were alive.

There was happiness among the People then. They built boats and one by one they went into the waters of the Stikine and down the mysterious wild canyon to their new home.

And so it was that the People became the people of the sea. They found the grandmothers and they built lodges to keep the children dry from the rain.

The men built great boats to go into the ocean, and the ocean gave the People its fish and its seals for food.

And today, children of the raven and the eagle, you wake up to taste the fog and look for the sun. You dip the salmon in the bowls of seal oil and you grow strong. Your music is the cry of the eagle and the raven as they find their food.

And you live where the trees are tall and hide the rich berries, and you live where the rain makes the world clean and the sting of the great cold is unknown.

You are now Raven's Children, but you should remember to tell your own children someday that it was not always so.

MY DEBUT AS
A FLY-FISHING
LEGEND

→

I t wasn't my fault. No self-respecting owner of a new (to him) Fenwick glass fly rod could postpone trying it out. It was just the way it all happened—hey, like an act of Nature, you know. A few children and grandchildren were embarrassed. But sometimes that's the price one must pay for becoming a fly-fishing legend in a small Alaska town.

My son-in-law had to work that first day we were in Haines. That was the basic problem, not me. If he had had the day off, he could've driven us up the seven miles to where the famous Chilkoot River pours out of Chilkoot Lake and runs its short mile or so before emptying into Lutak Inlet, part of the Lynn Canal, which is part of the Pacific Ocean.

And, oh, that first morning was glorious! In Haines, Alaska, this means foggy and rainy and dismal and just—well, wet and wonderful. I had gone to Haines to visit my daughter and her family, and to be a guest on a national radio program, plugging my latest Alaska novel, *Raven's Prey*. Alaska daughter Amanda Randles Stossel had set that up, as she was a reporter for KHNS, the little public radio station in Haines.

So I brought with me New Mexico daughter Bridget Randles, then about sixteen years old, who was visiting Alaska for the first time. Now I must admit that I was a bit more excited about heading back North than NMD was. After the first soggy day on the Alaska ferry, she was able to find more stimulation in books than in the scenery. Her father, on the other hand, was flickering around the ship like a crazy man, reliving wonderful memories of that verdant Southeast Alaska country. At one point, I recall going into the ship's lounge, where she was knee-deep in reading a teenage drama, and telling her she had to come out on the deck right then, because we were coming up on Kupreanof Island. She looked up at me as a dog would a bothersome mosquito.

"Don't tell me," she'd said, resignedly. "Let me guess. Kupreanof Island is a big, green, wet mountain coming out of the ocean and there are a lot of clouds around it."

I just nodded and left. So she's a lucky guesser, that's all.

So it was, after a couple of days and nights on the ship, that New Mexico Daughter and I were hugging Alaska Family in Haines and having a wonderful time. The problem was, the next day dawned gloriously wet and I had a fabulous Fenwick rod to try out, and I had no wheels and the fish were seven miles away through grizzly country.

After breakfast, I took the three-block walk, carrying the Fenwick, of course, and arrived at the small boat harbor in Haines. The harbor is on Lynn Canal, which is the longest fiord—eighty miles long—in North America, and is salt water. I had a freshwater fly rod and I didn't know how it handled. The way I looked at it then (and I still do because this thinking works for me, and I'm sticking with it) is that a man shouldn't wait until it's time to catch fish to try out a new rod. Oh no. Much better to practice casting and see how it operates before tackling fishing waters.

So I walked down to the harbor, right in front of a nice seafood restaurant full of locals, and started fishing. Oh, that Fenwick was sweet! I got to where I could turn that Royal Coachman over and put it right about where I wanted it, just to the left of that salmon trawler, or over to the front of that purse seiner. I was a veritable whirlwind of fly casting that morning, and I noticed, from time to time, that I had drawn something of an audience at the windows of the seafood restaurant.

So about noon, I packed up and trudged back up the three blocks to the house. Alaska Daughter was already there.

"It was *you*, wasn't it?" she said.

"What do you mean?" I asked, in all innocence.

"You were the nut in the red hat who was fly fishing in the Pacific Ocean, weren't you? We got phone calls at the station, but you know how people exaggerate."

"Now, honey," I said. "I had this new rod that I hadn't tried yet."

She grinned and shook her head. I was beginning to think I might survive this crisis.

"You know," she said. "This is a very small town. Sooner or later, someone's going to find out who you're related to."

"Blood will tell," I said.

So the next morning we all got up and piled in the car and son-in-law Paul drove us up to where the Chilkoot River comes out of one of the most beautiful lakes in the world. And the fish were biting. We set about filling Alaska Daughter's freezer with humpy salmon, and at the same time managed to catch a couple of really nice fat Dolly Vardens.

We did a bunch of subdividing, washing, and freezing of fish that morning, but left the Dolly Vardens in one piece for the time being.

That afternoon, I took the Fenwick and went back down to the boat harbor. In no time at all, I was laying some beautiful casts out there in the salt water, and naturally getting the same results I had gotten the day before: no fish, but a healthy (and growing) audience. The harbormaster emerged from his little cabin with binoculars and checked me out, and there seemed to be more people in the windows of the seafood restaurant. I wonder if I could've made a deal with the owners to get paid for bringing them more customers. I can't help it if I don't think of these things until later.

So, with my fan club already perched in the restaurant windows, I started moving slowly along the spit of land, casting as I went. In about ten minutes, I was out of sight of the restaurant windows, and I walked over through the woods a short ways where my daughters had brought me those two big Dolly Vardens. I waited for about fifteen minutes. Then, carrying the Dollys in plain sight, I walked around the bend and back in front of the restaurant windows with those freshwater fish and pretended to ignore the bugged eyes watching me go.

About an hour later, we were seated at this same restaurant and one kindly old sourdough came by the table. He was dying to say something about my apparent afternoon catch.

"I, uh, saw those fish you had there," he said. "Looks like the fishing was pretty good."

It was a question and not a statement, and I knew it.

I grinned up at him. "The fishing was even better this morning."

Well, that was certainly true. In such a manner does a guy become a fly-fishing legend in Haines, Alaska.

SITTIN'
RIGHT HERE
BY THE FIRE

———————————————————➤

Boys, I'm glad to see you back,
Down from the trail and the ridge and the track.
No deer? Well, that's all right, don't even perspire
Just grab a cup and join me here,
We don't need no dadgummed deer,
Just sittin' right here by the fire.

I started out today, same as you, eye to the mountain,
Climbing higher.
Then the lumbago got to fighting with my arthritis,
Scrappin' there inside us,
And I've found, since I retired,
That he also serves who sits and waits, and makes coffee
    for you boys,
And cooks some cobbler in that Dutch oven over there, and
        puts them little mints on your sleeping bags, and does up
        the breakfast dishes and then gets kinda tired, and that's
        why I'm sittin' right here,
Sittin' right here by the fire.

I guess I'm not sorry, really, that I stayed behind today.
See, I heard you, Bob, going chuff, chuff, chuffity chuff up
   Thompson Ridge.
Flat wore me out, it did, listening to your chuffer gettin'
   tired. You oughta get them lungs looked at, boy, or you'll
   expire. But I was rested up pretty good by then, just sittin'
   right here by the fire.

And you, Hank? Aw, you left here singin' like a thrush, but I
   could hear you crashin' through the brush,
Goin' up the draw,
Wearin' your patience raw.
Flip, crash, flip crash, bang crash, crash,
Just hearin' all your noisy walkin' made me tired,
So I thought I'd get myself another cup of coffee, just sittin'
   right here by the fire.

And George? Why, I heard you, too, sloppin' out through
   Seyfous Marsh, sounding obscene you were, pullin' each
   boot from the slop.
Suckity-clop, suckity suckity, suckity-clop you went,
Sounded like a bunch of eighth graders at a kissin' contest.
I don't think you could put a patented power sneak on a
   lawn mower.
So I just said what the heck, let the sun warm my neck, and
   kept sittin' right here by the fire.

Did I feel guilt? You know? With you boys out there chuffin'
   and thrashin' and suckity cloppin' 'round the woods?
To be honest, I thought on it, some. Those old shouldas came
   around. You know how they come . . . but they couldn't
   get no purchase. And by then I had to fetch some more
   wood, and that made me kinda tired.
I thought my Louis L'Amour book was pretty good,
   The words aren't long. I'm up to Chapter 3.

So the truth is, I just don't give a rat's dooly-dooly-doo
While I'm sittin' right here by the fire.

It ain't the way we're supposed to hunt, I know, but I thought
    you wouldn't mind much if I hung around camp and
    catered my desire.
And cooked some heart and kidney stew for you in that
    cast-iron twelve-incher next to the coffee on our nice
    little fire.
Aw heck, boys, you're more than welcome.
Pleasure's all mine. Not one more word!
I like doing this, you know. Gives me something to do.
And it really wasn't all that dull,
I had a little nap and all,
So it was okay, just sittin' and readin,' sippin' coffee
    and dozin,'
Eyes openin' and closin'
As that warm fall sun climbed higher.
And I was still sittin' right here by the fire.

Now I don't know if it was the chuff, chuff, chuffin' of Bob
    climbing higher, or the flip crash crash of Hank brush-
    thrashin,' or the suck-suckity suck-suckity of George
    traversin' the mire,
But one of you chased a big ol' buck right into camp here
    today, much to his dismay.
I looked at him and he looked at me and we had one of them
    hunter's moments, you know?
We had us an interesting situation, of course, where one of us
    was bound to be upset at the outcome.
I knew you boys and your ways, and knew you'd probably just
    call me a liar,
So I got my bow and helped him expire.

He's hangin,' yeah, right over behind Bob there in that tree.
Might oughta crank him a bit higher.
And tomorrow I'll be up to Chapter 4,
And see what ol' Louis has in store.
What mortal man could ask for more?
And you boys . . . you'll still be tired.
But I won't give a rat's dooly-dooly-doo, 'cause I'll
    be sittin' right here by the fire.

Breaking Camp

→

I t's like walking in cold gold now, with the hunters gone home. Gone is the anxiety over who will take a trophy animal home and who won't. Gone is the pressure to rise before daylight.

Now we get up when the sun gets up. We make quiet coffee and smile and walk outside into the cold of fall in the Jemez Mountains. Oh, we can't help taking the binoculars and looking off across the canyon of the San Antonio—what our hunters call the Hell Hole—to the other side where meadows sometimes hold early morning elk. Nothing there this morning. We smile, because there doesn't have to be any elk there this morning.

We look across at that mysterious tangled mountainside that held the legendary "Godzilla" bull in his final years. Now, of course, another bull, a younger bull, has moved in and is caring for the cows Godzilla left behind.

We go back into the tent and let the late fall light filter through the white canvas and warm us inside as the heat from the cast-iron stove warms us outside. We laugh now, remembering the season and the funny things that happened, and we smile for the new friends we've made in these mountains and for the old friends that keep us coming back each fall. As my friend George Cornell is fond of saying, "Remember, this isn't a rehearsal."

That's right. This is the real thing. Day after day. This is the life of an outdoorsman, with its sparkle, its pain, its disappointments, its victories, its fun and its laughter.

Daughter Bridget, who worked her way up from camp grunt to guide, is here to help break camp. So is Daughter Mandy, down from her home in Alaska to help with the guiding. And now her kids are becoming camp grunts. Doc and Susan have finished the season with us, too. The hunters will remember Susan's cooking long after they forget my name, and Doc's guiding is surpassed only by his sense of humor. But before it's all done, there will be one more night here first. Family night. Family and friends will come up and I'll whip something up in the Dutch oven, and we'll have some elk steaks and just sit tiredly and laugh and go to sleep early. The children and grandchildren will get to see what camp is like and have a day and night of fun, this camp that was sanctified with the burning of sweetgrass on its first morning each fall.

This afternoon I believe I'll walk up that canyon over there just to see if that big bull has come down yet. I waited on him through two hunters and wasn't able to get on him. But now, even after the close of the season, I just want to see if he goes through there. I want to walk on the crisp golden leaves of the aspen and feel the new bite of the winter to come. I want to flare my nostrils against the snap of the cold. Once more for the year I want to look for tracks, and glass the mountains for game, for we never know how many more mornings will be there for us.

Before this white canvas home becomes once again a large roll in a storage locker, I want to soak up the light coming through. I want to be at home here again next year, and the year after that.

Because we can never have too many days like this in our lives. We can't see the future, but we can savor the present, and what's more important, we can share the present.

This time tomorrow, here at the overlook, here at the Garita Gate, there won't be much left to show that we've made this our fall home. Oh, there's still the blackened rocks at the fire pit, just as they've been since before the Spanish came to these mountains. And there's that pile of firewood I'm leaving behind for the next guy. But otherwise, we'll say goodbye for another year with a clean camp and warm memories.

After all, what we are doing here is storing up memories and stories, for ourselves and for others, and that is the real treasure of the mountains. Those are the real trophies we take home with us when it's time to come in out of the cold.

ACKNOWLEDGMENTS

—————————————————————————————————▶

Thanks to the original publishers of some of the contents of this book.

"The Day the Mountains Flipped Over," "Thirty Feet from Death," "The Ballad of Nimrod Bodfish," "Remember . . . Forest Fires Prevent Bears," "The Dancing Mukluks," and "Raven's Children" are reprinted courtesy of Marqcom Media from *Strange Tales of Alaska*.

"Going to the High Country," "I Need Coffee," "Stinkin' Skunk," and "Soaked in Summer" were first published in *New Mexico Magazine*.

"Dave's Bear" first appeared in *The Long Dark*, first published by Alaska Northwest Publishing and reissued by McRoy & Blackburn.

"Jeep and the Grandfathers" is from *Raven's Prey*, published by McRoy & Blackburn.

"Trouble on Trail" is an excerpt from *Dogsled: A True Tale of the North*, published by Winchester Press.

"Think Before You Stink" comes from "Dancing Through Dark Timber: A Commonsense Approach to Elk Hunting" (not yet published).

"Night Ride" was previously published in *Hot Biscuits*, and "A Return to the Saddle" and "The Buckskin Stud" appeared in *Sun Dog Days*, both books published by the University of New Mexico Press.

ABOUT THE
AUTHOR

S lim Randles writes a syndicated newspaper column, "Home Country," and is the author of many books, among them *Sun Dog Days*, *Ol' Max Evans*, and *Ol' Slim's Views from the Porch*, all three available from the University of New Mexico Press. He lives in Albuquerque, New Mexico, and may be reached at www.slimrandles.com.